Damage Limitation:
trying to reduce the harm schools do to children

by Roland Meighan

with contributions by Linda Brown,
Hazel Clawley, Charlie Cooper,
Jane Dent, Clive Erricker, Kim Evans,
Michael Foot, Derry Hannam,
Clive Harber, Ben Koralek,
and Philip Toogood

A briefing book on how to get educated despite school

Published 2004 by Educational Heretics Press
113 Arundel Drive, Bramcote, Nottingham NG9 3FQ

Copyright © 2004 Educational Heretics Press

British Cataloguing in Publication Data

Meighan, Roland
    Damage Limitation:
    Trying to reduce the harm schools do to children
    1.School psychology 2.School environment 3.Students –
    Psychology 4.Psychological child abuse 5.Psychological
    child abuse – Prevention 6.Learning, Psychology of
I.Title
371.7'1

ISBN   **1-900219-27-1**

This book is sold subject to the condition that it shall not, by way of trade or otherwise, be lent, re-sold, hired out, or otherwise circulated without the publisher's prior consent in any form of binding or cover other than that in which it is published and without a similar condition being imposed on the subsequent purchasers.

Design and production: Educational Heretics Press

Cover design by Educational Heretics Press

Printed by NPM Ltd., Riverside Road, Pride Park, Derby

Contributors

Linda Brown is a former first school head teacher

Hazel Clawley is an experienced home-based educator

Charlie Cooper is a researcher and lecturer at the University of Hull

Jane Dent is an experienced home-based educator

Clive Erricker is County Inspector for Religious Education, Hampshire

Kim Evans is a former local government official with a life-long interest in education and an M.Ed from the Open University

Michael Foot is a retired primary school head teacher

Derry Hannam is a researcher into democratic forms of education

Clive Harber is Professor of Education, University of Birmingham

Ben Koralek is a former primary school teacher and Director of SHAPE at the Built Environment Centre in the East of England Region.

Philip Toogood is a former secondary school head teacher

Contents

Foreword

Preface

Part one:	**Damage limitation**	**1**
Part two:	**The point of view of the learners**	**12**
Part three:	**Learn your lines, or, stay a victim of compulsory mis-education**	**24**
Part four:	**The point of view of the parents**	**37**
Part five:	**Grandparents**	**49**
Part six:	**Teachers trying to make their classrooms more learner-friendly places**	**56**
Part seven:	**Damage Limitation: the Do-it-yourself Approach**	**73**
Part eight:	**Schooling can seriously damage your health: education for violence, education for peace**	**81**
Postscript		**95**

Foreword

I have spent almost fifty years in schools: first as a pupil, then as a teacher, an education officer and a County adviser. Now I am a school governor. But I do not look forward to the prospect of going into schools any more.

I have to take a deep breath and I have to put on a positive, cheerful demeanour, for I know that 1 will have to look the system full in the face, every visit, and I know that it will make me unutterably sad.

Why? Why will my walk down the corridor and my visit to the classroom and my attendance at a Governors' meeting make me so unhappy? And why has the recent OFSTED inspection of our secondary school – an expensive charade played out before a captive audience - driven me to speechless levels of impotent anger?

Why does my heart sink when I read of the pupils temporarily and permanently excluded? Why can't I rejoice in the school's strategies to improve the exam results? Why can't I rejoice in the school's strategies to improve the attendance rates, and in its strategies to stamp out bullying and in its policies on the wearing of school uniform and the control of litter? Why can't I rejoice in the knowledge that, after a few days' presence, the OFSTED team consulted its tick lists and concluded that a high percentage of the lessons observed were 'satisfactory'?

I cannot.

As I walk down the corridors now and sit in on lessons and attend Governors' meetings, I see and hear from the imprisoned, the deflected, the exhausted and often the deflated. I find myself particularly studying the Headteacher for any sign of his or her cracking up, or giving up. Amazingly, despite everything, some enthusiasms do survive in small places and small doses.

But all is not well. Almost every week now I read of changes in the educational policy of the government, and these changes add up to an unacknowledged admission that things have gone badly wrong.

As I write, I have on my desk some news of the latest change: national trials are under way, apparently, of a new and less stressful test for seven-year-olds in England. The head of testing at the Qualifications and Curriculum Authority has said: *"I think this is the future, if we are going to move away from high stakes testing. We want to see if the current system can be improved, above all by valuing the teacher's detailed knowledge of the children in the class."*

What words! What sentiments! Shall we weep now, or later? The damage already done to seven-year-olds by key stage one testing is quietly buried beneath another vision of the future for young children in the schools they have to attend. The damage is real. This book makes that abundantly clear; so powerfully clear in fact, that one could be forgiven for doing a Corporal Jones, who, whenever a threatening situation occurs, runs around exhorting people not to panic.

The contributors to *Damage Limitation* offer an alternative to panic, and an alternative to formal schooling. They are not siren voices. Far from it. They look at the present system of schooling with a clear, unflinching eye, and suggest what should happen to make schools, which are by their very nature authoritarian institutions having to march to a tune not of their own making, far less damaging to children. In addition, they go on to unfold their belief in children, in how children learn and in how they should be treated. They declare their belief in the life-affirming purpose of education, and in doing so they refuse to accept that there is no alternative to what John Taylor Gatto calls the 'twelve year jail sentence'.

As a briefing book on how to get educated despite school, this is both a timely exposure and a heart-warming inspiration. It is written by people whose experience in education has touched them deeply, and made them think long and hard about what it means, and what it takes, to be educated. It deserves to be read by as wide an audience as possible, and we owe Professor Meighan a debt of gratitude for bringing it to life.

Peter Holt
Senior County Adviser (Retired), Norfolk

Preface

For 'education, education, education', read 'schooling, schooling, schooling'

I need to start by pointing out that this book is not an attack on individual teachers, who often try to make their classrooms as learner-friendly as the circumstances, over which they have little control, will allow. Instead it is an exposure of the learning system that has been imposed upon us by those members of the ruling elite with persistent totalitarian tendencies, who prefer a controlled population to an educated one.

It is, after all, a learning system from last century devised in the previous century to cope with an information-poor society and the needs of industrialisation. Even during the last century it was described as 'compulsory mis-education' (Paul Goodman), 'the tragedy of education' (Edmond Holmes), 'the betrayal of youth' (James Hemming) and 'compulsory schooling disease' (Chris Shute).

The current situation now shames us all. I never thought, as a young teacher starting out in 1959, I would live to see:

- a parent sent to prison because the children were too unhappy at school to attend
- a teacher sent to prison for cheating in examinations
- head teachers dismissed for cheating
- a school that refused the SATs 'fined' £3000 of their annual allocation until they caved in
- cases of teachers taking their own lives because of the oppressiveness of the inspection service, OFSTED
- a teacher setting fire to a school, joining the ranks of pupils who do so
- police patrols to round up school refusers
- a proposal that head teachers issue £50 fines to parents in respect of truancy
- head teachers to fine parents up to £100 for taking their children away on holiday in term time without permission
- about a third of all teachers wishing to leave teaching as soon as possible

- 31% of young parents with pre-school age children having so little regard for schools that they are considering home-based education. And, 61% of these not long after experiencing the system for themselves, saying they have little trust in the education system to provide a decent education. *(Vauxhall Centenary Parents Survey, 2002)*

Recently, random drug testing has been added to the list. Any one of these facts taken individually might not signify much, but taken together they indicate that something is fundamentally wrong with the current learning system which is based on 'children in captivity' type schooling, using coercion and heavy with domination.

These are the characteristics of the learning systems of totalitarian societies. In contrast, it was Nelson Mandela's choice for his Minister of Education, Professor Bengu, who declared that 'democracy means the **absence** of domination'.

A radical change is needed for a modern learning system fit for a democracy. It needs to get away from domination and its endless stream of uninvited teaching. Instead it needs to be **personalised** in the sense of being learner-managed, based on invitation and encouragement and, if we actually believe in life-long learning, **non-ageist**. It needs to be **democratic** in at least three aspects - its organisation for participation rather than imposition, its monitoring procedures for the **celebration of learning** rather than incessant and stultifying testing, and in its adoption of the more natural 'catalogue' curriculum approach.

For the benefit of those who think this all just impossible dreams, we already have a democratic learning institution in our midst based on these principles. It is called the public library system. There are others, such as museums, nursery centres, home-based education networks/co-operatives and community arts programmes. So we already know how to make such systems work. I even know just a few schools that are attempting to work to these principles, as far as the mass coercive system allows. The most successful form of genuine education available for children at present, however, is home-based education, and, unsurprisingly, these families usually make a bee-line for their local democratic learning institution – the public library.

The present domination-riddled learning system is the result of the *Great Leap Backwards* of 1988 when the Thatcher government, after a power struggle in the Cabinet between traditionalists in the Department for Education and futurists in the Department for Employment led by David Young, took us back in time to the kind of schooling system of the early 1900s. The discredited idea of a National Curriculum, endless testing and aggressive inspection was re-established, and later amplified by the New Labour group of people with their brand of totalitarian tendencies.

The first National Curriculum along with its repressive trappings of testing and aggressive inspection, had eventually been discarded after the Chief Inspector for Schools, Edmond Holmes, wrote a book declaring it *The Tragedy of Education* in 1921. This was the system Holmes saw as stultifying teachers, debasing teaching and learning, inducing cheating by linking funding to test results, and weakening imagination, creativity, and flexibility, whilst promoting *"a profound misconception of the meaning of life"* by replacing improvement, through encouragement and co-operation, with ruthless competition and the allocation of blame for 'failure'.

If Britain wanted to have an education system fit for a new century, he concluded, it would have to stop telling children what to do and compelling them to do it, since this produced only passivity, lassitude, unhealthy docility or, in the stronger, more determined spirits, 'naughtiness'. Teaching had become a debased activity:

"In nine schools out of ten, on nine days out of ten, in nine lessons out of ten, the teacher is engaged in laying thin films of information on the surface of the child's mind and then after a brief interval he is skimming these off in order to satisfy himself that they have been duly laid."
Holmes, E. (1911) *What Is, and What Might Be*, p.56

The view of Holmes, as well as being similar to that of the 31% of young parents mentioned earlier, was echoed by Bertrand Russell:

"There must be in the world many parents who, like the present author, have young children whom they are anxious to educate as well as possible, but reluctant to expose to the evils of existing educational institutions." (*On Education*, 1926, page 7)

The answer to the question of what is wrong with mass, coercive schooling is 291. That is the number of separate criticisms logged by Nigel Wright in his Ph.D. research, even before the advent of the second National Curriculum, league tables and obsessive testing. This could be taken to mean that there are 291 possible ways that children can be harmed.

Some families are able to escape the damage by undertaking home-based education. Others find one of the few learner-friendly democratic small schools. A few manage to achieve a flexi-time school contract. But most, by force of circumstances, have to make use of schools. This book explores, for them, some of the possibilities for limiting the damage. For, as Winston Churchill pointed out: *"Schools have not necessarily much to do with education ... they are mainly institutions of control where certain basic habits must be instilled in the young. Education is quite different and has little place in school"*. Sadly, he did not go on to question whether such places have any legitimacy in a democracy at all.

The **learner-hostile** nature of our current school system is indicated in the classic anthropological study of classrooms, *Life in Classrooms*, by Philip Jackson when he concluded that, for all the children some of the time, and for some of the children all of the time, the classroom resembles a cage from which there is no escape. It is echoed in Colin Ward's comment that our expenditure on teachers and plant is mostly wasted by attempting to teach people what they do not want to learn in a situation that they would rather not be involved in.

The alternative pathway for teachers is as 'guides on the side' with minimal use of the 'sage on the stage', of learner-directed learning rather than teacher-directed, of the catalogue curriculum not the government-devised curriculum. Some of these ideas have been developed in the work of John Adcock in his recent books *In Place of Schools* and *Teaching Tomorrow*.

The absurdity of trying to defend the present obsolete, counter-productive and rights-abusing learning system was shown in a head teacher's desperate outburst to some doubting parents, *"If only you would make your home less interesting, your children would not be so bored at school"*. Such parents are forced to adopt the advice of Mark Twain – never let schooling interfere with your education! But we could devise a learning system that was education and not schooling.

The harm done by such a system is often subtle, largely unrecognised and cumulative, as Edmond Holmes was at pains to point out:

> *"For, with the best of intentions, the leading actors in it, the parents and teachers of each successive generation, so bear themselves as to entail never-ending calamities on the whole human race - not the sensational calamities which dramatists love to depict, but inward calamities which are the deadlier for their very unobtrusiveness, for our being so familiar with them that we accept them at last as our appointed lot - such calamities as perverted ideals, debased standards, contracted horizons, externalised aims, self-centred activities, weakened will-power, lowered vitality, restricted and distorted growth, and (crowning and summarising the rest) a profound misconception of the meaning of life."*
>
> Holmes, E. (1911) in *What Is, and What Might Be*

US writer Nat Needle picks up on the 'profound misconception of the meaning of life' eighty seven years later. In contrast to the view that the victors in the 'strong versus weak' battle deserve our adulation for setting the pace for the rest of us, Needle reminds us of another view. It is that the strongest are those who devote themselves to strengthening the weak, to keeping the whole community afloat, to ploughing their gifts back into the common field through service to others. He concludes,

> *"I don't care to motivate my children by telling them that they will have to be strong to survive the ruthless competition. I'd rather tell them that the world needs their wisdom, their talents, and their kindness, so much so that the possibilities for a life of service are without limits of any kind. I'd like to share with them the open secret that this is the path to receiving what one needs in a lifetime, and to becoming strong."*
>
> Nat Needle in AERO-Gramme (number 25, Fall 1998)

As governments world-wide bang the drum for more education, Don Glines of *Educational Futures Projects*, USA, introduces a sobering thought that might have appealed to Edmond Holmes:

"... the majority of the dilemmas facing society have been perpetrated by the best traditional college graduates: environmental pollution; political ethics; have/have not gap; under-employment - (in fact) the sixty four micro-problems which equal our one macro-problem!"

If some of the highly literate are responsible for many of the major problems that now face the world, perhaps we need less 'education' and more 'wisdom'? Or perhaps we need a quite different kind of education?

If you want to produce people with democratic habits, discipline and understanding, or self-directing and self-managing people, then you will need to adopt a learning system that will do this. Thus, a current mistake in UK is the citizenship initiative, believing that **preaching** the virtues of democracy from within an authoritarian learning system will do the trick. It fails to work, and can be counter-productive in producing cynicism. South Africa, in adopting various measures to democratise its schools, has displayed much more wisdom.

The authoritarian model of education underpinning our schooling system usually spawns bully institutions and behaviour. As I wrote in an article for *Natural Parent* magazine:

*"School, based on the current model of the compulsory day-prison, is itself **a bully institution**. Next it employs **a bully curriculum** - the compulsory National Curriculum. This is enforced by the increasingly favoured **bully pedagogy** of teacher-dominated formal teaching. Currently this is reinforced by the **bully compulsory assessment system**. The unwritten, but powerful message of this fourfold package, is this: adults get their way by bullying, psychological, institutional or otherwise.*

"There are at least three types of outcome. The 'successful' pupils grow up to be officially sanctioned bullies in dominant authority positions as assertive politicians, doctors, teachers, civil servants, journalists and the like who are lukewarm or dismissive about democratic behaviour. A majority of the 'less successful' learn to accept the mentality of the bullied - the submissive and dependent mind-set of people who need someone to tell them what to think and do. A third outcome is the production of a group of free-lance bullies who first

> become active in the underworld of schools and then end up in trouble of varying degrees of seriousness.
>
> "Until we replace this morbid model with a new model of an 'invitational' learning system based on democratic principles and operating within a flexible education system, the root causes of bullying will continue."

But, John Holt forecast in 1975 that there was a desire for schools to be even more rigid, threatening, and punitive than they are, and they will probably become so. How right he was! Those with totalitarian tendencies have had their way for some time now.

Moreover, we do not have to get sentimental about parents. Although many may recognise the analysis so far, others will have absorbed the superstitions of mass, coercive schooling and the usual totalitarian excuse, *"it is for their own good"*. Indeed, according to public opinion surveys, about half UK parents would return to hitting children with canes as a means of punishment, by bringing back corporal punishment. Some, as John Holt pointed out, are just fatalistic, seeing the world as a nasty place which they cannot see being changed for the better, so it is best to get the children brutalized ('toughened up') to cope with it. Bullying children into compliance is just seen as 'necessary'. And, with a little bit of luck, some might even rise up to the upper layers of the heap and get some of the 'prizes'.

It may be some time before we have a decent learning system which is learner-friendly, personalised, flexible and democratic and based on the principles of 'anybody, any age; any time, any place; any pathway, any pace'. In the meantime, this book explores the possibilities of damage limitation.

I would like to express my appreciation to the eleven other educational heretics who have contributed to this book and thus helped extend its scope, and hopefully, its impact.

Roland Meighan

Part one:

Damage limitation

by Roland Meighan

Just when you think life holds no more surprises, something odd happens. Recently, I was in the middle of giving a talk on natural learning to a large group of parents and grandparents when they suddenly burst into applause - this has never happened to me before. What was it that had touched the nerve? Well, I had just read out a statement by E.T. Hall about what schools do to children:

"Schools have transformed learning from one of the most rewarding of all human activities into a painful, boring, dull, fragmenting, mind-shrinking, soul-shriveling experience."

These parents and grandparents were very unhappy about the system of mass, coercive schooling and what it was achieving, and many of them came to talk to me afterwards about their relief at hearing someone articulate their misgivings. The problems with mass coercive schooling, they agreed, are that it is, (a) mass not personalised, (b) coercive not invitational, (c) schooling not education.

During the session I had reminded them about Winston Churchill's verdict. Churchill has recently been voted in a popularity competition as the 'greatest Englishman ever' (although my vote would have gone to Tom Paine), and so he might be thought to be someone with wise opinions. He proposed that:

"Schools have not necessarily much to do with education ... they are mainly institutions of control where certain basic habits must be instilled in the young. Education is quite different and has little place in school."

Churchill did not reflect further, that this meant that schools were (a) an obsolete institution, (b) counter-productive in a democracy, and (c) an abuse of three or four human rights. Tom Paine as author of *The Rights of Man* and of the original USA Constitution, would probably have done so, had he been in Churchill's place.

Natural learning and how it is hijacked

I arrived at Charmouth in Dorset on a sunny Saturday afternoon in May, and went down to the beach with Janet to take in the scene. It was the start of a week-long festival and conference for home-based educating families and about 1500 people of all ages would be in attendance. I was due to start the conference with a keynote presentation on *'Natural Learning and the Natural Curriculum'* but I was not yet clear how to set the scene. But for now, relaxing on the beach just seemed to be a good idea.

We gazed with interest at the scene in front of us. Two young surfers were developing their skills on their miniature surf-boards on the incoming waves. Beyond them two young canoeists were in action. Two younger children were enjoying jumping the waves as they petered out near the edge of the beach, the smaller one sensibly retreating if a slightly larger wave came in.

Three adults went in front of us and paused at a pictorial display on local fossils, enjoyed talking about it for a minute or two and then went on their way. Along the beach a young boy of about eleven years was working with what appeared to be his grandfather on the fossil beach. Somebody else was reading a book.

Other people of all ages were swimming, paddling and making sandcastles. One young group had not yet got the sand mix right and their sandcastles kept crumbling. But with trial and error they solved the problem. Parents were on hand everywhere generally keeping a watchful eye but not interfering unduly. A rock pipit appeared close to us and we spent a little time observing it and talking about its appearance and behaviour.

Everyone seemed relaxed and happy and nobody was infringing the rights of others to be doing their own thing – a miniature display of democracy in action, as diversity and variety were cheerfully celebrated. It was also a demonstration of natural learning and the natural curriculum, whilst it illustrated the sub-title of my talk to open the conference: *'anybody, any age; any time, any place; any pathway, any pace.'* There was no sign of any 'uninvited teaching' anywhere to be seen.

Then we began to speculate what a guardian of 'unnatural learning', an OFSTED inspector perhaps, would have to say about the same scene. Well, as regards the surfboarders, there was no sign of professional input. No trained teacher was present to set appropriate tasks, attainment targets and tests. The same applied to the canoeists who did not seem to be working to a graded plan of skill development.

The young ones were enjoying jumping the waves but was this preparing them for their baseline assessment? The adults were rather casual about the fossil display as no follow-up work appeared to be in evidence.

The grandfather and child were from quite different 'key-stages', if key-stages had yet been devised for grandfathers. The book and newspaper readers seemed very casual about their chosen tasks and put down their book or newspaper whenever they felt like it. And was the book on the approved list for study anyway?

A decent teacher would have had a rock pipit workcard for when the bird appeared so that appropriate written work could be undertaken. There was no sign of a literacy hour or a numeracy hour to be seen. It was all rather amateur.

So, out of the conversation with Janet, the beach scene could be seen as an interesting example of natural learning in action. I had my introduction: 'on the beach'.

The rise of the 'miserable rule-followers'

Almost everyone starts out with hopes and even high hopes of going to school. Children may anticipate entry into a world of interest, stimulation and development. Teachers may anticipate a worthwhile, satisfying and positive occupation. Parents hope for the blossoming of their children. Grandparents may anticipate happy grandchildren growing up positively in the world.

But it all seems to go wrong somewhere. Firstly, teachers can end up reporting that *"We are just miserable rule-followers ..."*. This is the verdict of a teacher in South Africa, reported by Clive Harber in *State of Transition*, London: Symposium Books, 2001. But it could be anywhere in the world, given Edward de Bono's verdict that **all the schooling systems he has encountered in the world are a disgrace.**

I have to agree, for all the ones I have encountered are also a disgrace, although some are larger disasters and some are smaller ones. Only a few anywhere are trying to be more democratic and are concerned to be less constipated and less learner-hostile in their approach, by having a just a few echoes of natural learning. Not surprisingly, the *'miserable rule-followers'* are currently leaving teaching in droves and in disgust, and many who stay explain that they would leave if they could.

Then, children have their hopes dashed too. As early as age six they can already be reporting that they are aware that their minds are being hijacked. They recognise that their concerns, their interests, their agendas, are already being systematically squeezed off the school's agenda. But they feel powerless to do anything about it and are already, at six years of age, reconciled to having to conform to a script written by remote others. They, too, become *'just miserable rule-followers'*. (See research by Ann Sherman (1996) *Rules, Routines and Regimentation*, Nottingham: Educational Heretics Press)

Next, many parents may have their desires thwarted. They may begin to report that school is not doing the kind of things they had hoped. They may find they have handed their children over, in good faith, to a bunch of strangers, hoping for the best, but getting something undesirable – a deadening of the spirit. Some can take action and educate at home as a better option, others are forced by circumstances to become 'miserable rule-followers'. Some can try damage-limitation. Some persevere hoping to find treasure in the wreck.

'The Boulevard of Broken Dreams'
This experience of disillusionment is, in the words of the song title, *The Boulevard of Broken Dreams*. High hopes gradually – and sometimes very suddenly – become shattered. Schooling may then become what has sometimes been described as a long-sentence of suffering, endurance and general low-level misery. Some learn to put up with it, and even exploit it, better than others. **We should congratulate those teachers, and even whole schools, who manage, despite the odds, to keep some kind of oasis going in the general desert.** But it is the long landscapes of desert that I am writing about.

One of the propositions of my book, *Natural Learning and the Natural Curriculum*, is that this fate of becoming 'just miserable rule-followers' is one consequence of abandoning **natural** learning and the **natural** curriculum. In its place has been imposed false and shallow learning and the false, largely junk curriculum of the state – 'unnatural' learning and the 'unnatural' curriculum.

Paul Goodman described this as *Compulsory Mis-education* in his book. Chris Shute calls it *Compulsory Schooling Disease* in his. The Chief Inspector of Schools, Edmond Holmes, writing at the start of the 20th century, called it *The Tragedy of Education*.

The question of damage limitation: and can 'organic' toxin-free learning be a reality?
Every parent is a home-based educator until children approach the age of 5. After that, all parents are still home-based educators, although some are full-time, whereas others use schools for part of the time, during the weekdays, on those weeks the schools are open. For those who either choose to use schools, or necessity forces them to, I want to open up the question of damage limitation.

I had to face this question when, some years ago now, my son reached the age of 5. His mother, Shirley, was an experienced infants teacher, and I was an experienced secondary teacher and teacher educator. With our insider knowledge, we both understood the serious limitations of compulsory mass schooling, state or private, and set out to offer him a home-based education alternative. Ironically, he elected to try school, so his parents had to turn their attention to mounting a damage limitation programme.

Why was this necessary? A few years ago I wrote an article entitled 'Schooling can seriously damage your education'. I now think I was too cautious and should have entitled it, 'Schooling **will** damage your education'. **The only question in my mind is how much damage will be done and in which dimensions.**

There is **some** good news about schooling, however, as Everett Reimer indicated when he wrote, *"some true educational experiences are bound to occur in schools. They occur however, despite school and not because of it"*. Some teachers manage, despite our domination-riddled schooling system, to swim against the tide of restrictions and regulations, and create episodes of genuine humanity and genuine learning. I tried to be such a teacher and so do many others.

As my son put it, the good news was that he was able to find *"bits of treasure in the wreck"* of the schooling system, because of such teachers. But it is in the end, an illusion that makes us think something can be done to make schools educational, whereas the default position is always anti-democratic domination.

It is also true that the homes of some children are despotic or neglectful, so that even a coercive school can provide a respite. Schools also provide a respite for parents from their children, so that they can pursue their careers, or voluntary work, or hobbies, or sports, or whatever.

Compulsory mis-education

But the long-term effect of mass, compulsory coercive schooling is **damage**. As the New York prize-winning teacher, John Gatto put it, he was employed to teach bad habits. These ranged from bad intellectual habits, bad social habits, bad emotional habits, to bad moral and political habits. Neither the 'successful' pupils nor the 'unsuccessful' pupils escaped. For starters, he identified seven of these bad habits.

John Taylor Gatto recognised that what he was really paid to teach was an unwritten curriculum made up of seven ideas. The first was **confusion**. He was required to teach disconnected facts not meaning, infinite fragmentation not cohesion. The second basic idea was **class position**. Children were to be taught to know their place by being forced into the rigged competition of schooling. A third lesson was that of **indifference**. He saw he was paid to teach children not to care too much about anything. The lesson of bells is that no work is worth finishing: students never have a complete experience for it is all on the instalment plan.

The fourth lesson was that of **emotional dependency** for, by marks and grades, ticks and stars, smiles and frowns, he was required to teach children to surrender their wills to authority. The next idea to be passed on was that of **intellectual dependency**. They must learn that good people wait for an expert to tell them what to do and believe. The sixth idea is that of **provisional self-esteem**. Self-respect is determined by what others say about you in reports and grades; you are *told* what you are worth and self-evaluation is ignored. The final, seventh lesson is that **you cannot hide**. You are watched constantly and privacy is frowned upon.

The consequence of teaching the seven lessons is a growing indifference to the adult world, to the future, to most things except the diversion of toys, computer games, 'getting stoned' as the height of having a good time, and, for some, involvement in petty crime, hooliganism and violence.

School, Gatto concludes, is a twelve-year jail sentence where bad habits are the only curriculum truly learned. School 'schools' very well but it hardly educates at all. Indeed, Paul Goodman entitled his book *Compulsory Mis-education*. But all this is good preparation for being gullible to the other controlling institutions, such as universities, but especially television. This theme is developed in Gatto's book, *Dumbing Us Down: the hidden curriculum of compulsory schooling*.

In contrast, home-based education can be seen as analogous to organic farming – a system with the toxins avoided. As parents, our desire for 'damage limitation', however, meant 'building up the immune system' to fight the toxins of the schooling system.

Other parents were puzzled as to why we saw what they regarded as 'good' schools, which today would no doubt get OFSTED approval, as **'educational impoverishment zones'**. *"A good uniform means a good school",* they declared. *"And probably a bad education based on uniformity",* we responded. John Gatto had an explanation for the puzzled response of the parents: *"It is the great triumph of compulsory government monopoly mass-schooling that ... only a small number can imagine a different way to do things."*

So what did our policy of damage limitation look like? The first item was a principle: we would never pretend the school was right when it was wrong. If it proved necessary and with our son's approval, we would take the trouble to challenge the school when it was in the wrong, even if this meant we were labelled 'nuisance', 'interfering', or 'bad' parents. Part of this principle was never to shirk a dialogue with our son about what was happening in school and its implications. Thus, when a teacher, unable to find a guilty party, punished the whole class, we pointed out that this was a common fascist procedure, but also why the authoritarian system pushed teachers into this particular corner.

The second item was a positive programme of activities to offset some of the bad habits John Gatto identified. To some extent, we just continued the programme of activities used between the ages of zero and five years, providing a learner-friendly environment that was personalised and democratic, stressing fun and happiness. This involved construction toys, board games, electronic games, watching TV programmes together, playing games in the garden or park - business as usual in fact.

In addition, we located out-of-school clubs and activities such as judo groups, holiday soccer coaching courses, holiday table tennis events, and provided transport for groups of friends to go skating in the evening. One 'bit of treasure in the wreck' was the Local Education Authority's Saturday morning orchestra facility. This encouraged young musicians to gain experience with their own or with loaned instruments, in beginner ensembles and, eventually, in the senior orchestra. The LEA also had an Outdoor Centre in Wales and an Arts Residential Centre which were sources of worthwhile week-long courses.

The local naturalist society had regular Sunday outings to gardens, arboretums, bird watching sites ranging from woodland, to moorland, to seashore - even to sewage farms where we could view birds such as black terns – all in the company of enthusiasts. On occasion, we found ourselves at the Gibraltar Point Field Station for a weekend of investigation where father gained 'brownie points' for being the first to notice a rare red-backed shrike. The *I Spy* booklets were a useful cheap resource but another favourite purchase was the magazine, *The Puzzler*. We found that one of those magazines for young people which builds into a junior encyclopaedia was well worthwhile.

We organised our own day trips to seaside, to parks with funfairs, to houses, to cities and museums, to sporting events ranging from the local soccer and cricket teams to the world table tennis championships. There were National Car Shows and the Birmingham Show to experience. We involved ourselves in a local amateur dramatic society that welcomed children to help out backstage. Also, the family, including grandparents, would often come along to meet the families, when I was researching home-based education. There were package holidays abroad, to Sweden to visit friends and also to Spain.

Perhaps none of this seems all that remarkable, and families across the social range do some selection of these things, according to their means and inclinations. But we consciously saw all these activities as opportunities for purposive conversation and mutual learning and an antidote to the effects of schooling. We could try to provide holistic and integrated learning to offset the fragmented approach of the school, and use any opportunities to practice the democratic skills of negotiation, consultation, accommodation, and co-operation - the skills that authoritarian schools usually discount and discourage.

What was achieved? Well, perhaps partial success could be claimed. Just choosing to be at school, rather than being there by coercion, transformed the experience for our 'home-education truant'. At seven years of age, our son was telling us that, *"school did not get to him like the others, because he had an escape tunnel ready and waiting"*. At eleven, he went to the Open Day at the secondary school where 300 children from the feeder schools in the district were in attendance, but he was conscious of being the only one making a decision whether to go or not. **The others were conscripts.** Later, we saw the head teacher where my son informed him that he was giving the school a term's contract to see how things went. I came to realise that my son regarded the school in the same way that an anthropologist regards a tribe being studied – he was in the role of a participant observer.

The switch from school to further education college was eventually a considerable release from the domination of schooling. Independence of spirit and mind were better able to flourish.

On the other hand, moving away to university meant that this institution just had a field day. The intellectual dependence Gatto talks about now asserted itself in the form of courses and modules requiring replication of approved material and rejecting any alternative or independent analysis as a threat to the authority of 'experts'. We could only hope that some of our efforts at building up an intellectual immune system would pay off.

During twenty years working in universities, this continued intellectual dependence is what I observed happening as a matter of course, and pointing it out in committees was never well received. But it led me into devising a democratic learning co-operative approach as an attempted antidote.

Is a damage limitation policy really necessary? And does every parent using schools need one? John Stuart Mill in *On Liberty* (1859) p.177, observed that:

"A general State Education is a mere contrivance for moulding people to be exactly like one another, and as the mould in which it casts them is that which pleases the

dominant power in the government, whether this be a monarchy, an aristocracy, or a majority of the existing generation ... it establishes a despotism over the mind, leading by a natural tendency to one over the body."

This seems to me to be (a) just as true now as in 1859 and just as anti-democratic, and (b) just the opposite of an 'organic, toxin-free learning' outcome. In the film *Iris*, Iris Murdoch is portrayed as saying that the most important freedom is freedom of the mind. She lost this because of a wasting disease – Alzheimer's. Children are likely to lose it during schooling in exchange for becoming a dependent learner.

Part two:

The point of view of the learners: 15,000 children reporting on 15,000 hours of schooling

by Roland Meighan

In June 2001 the *Guardian* repeated an exercise first undertaken in the *Observer* in 1967 under the title of *The School That I'd Like*. Both studies explode the myth that children are happy with their schools. This myth is sustained by a steady stream of poor research that asks children loaded questions. When released from these by asking the simple but radical question, *"What kind of school would you like?"* the clear answer is *"Not the one we already have!"* In the original study, the only satisfied customers were a few learners who contributed to the essay competition who were educated at home.

Even the question *"What kind of school would you like?"* is loaded because it presumes school, operating on the current 'children in captivity' basic principle, is the only option. *"What kind of education would you like?"* would have been less restricting on the imagination. So the summariser, Dea Birkett, tells us: *"No-one proposed no school, although many did suggest less school. (Jonathan Adams wanted to 'have a free three days a month development leave where one can take time off school for just being an adolescent. Not having to explain!')"* What did she expect given such a loaded question?

The results are presented as:

The Children's Manifesto

We, the schoolchildren of Britain, have been given a voice. This is what we say: The school we would like is:
- **A beautiful school** with glass dome roofs to let in the light, uncluttered classrooms and brightly coloured walls.

- **A comfortable school** with sofas and beanbags, cushions on the floor, tables that do not scrape our knees, blinds that keep out the sun, and quiet rooms where we can chill out.
- **A safe school** with swipe cards for the school gate, anti-bully alarms, first aid classes, and someone to talk to about our problems.
- **A listening school** with children on the governing body, class representatives and the chance to vote for teachers.
- **A flexible school** without rigid timetables or exams, without compulsory homework, without a one-size-fits-all curriculum, so we can follow our own interests and spend more time on what we enjoy.
- **A relevant school** where we learn through experience, experiments and exploration, with trips to historic sites and teachers who have practical experience of what they teach.
- **A respectful school** where we are not treated like empty vessels to be filled with information, where teachers treat us as individuals, where children and adults can talk freely to each other, and our opinion matters.
- **A school without walls** so we can go outside to learn, with animals to look after and wild gardens to explore.
- **A school for everybody** with boys and girls from all backgrounds and abilities, with no grading, so we do not compete against each other but just do our best.

Damage limitation

Looking at this from a damage-limitation point of view, the message the young learners are giving us is clear – do not expect any of the above things to be in place. Learners who attend schools may well have to develop strategies to cope with some, if not all, of the following :

- **An ugly building** with indifferent lighting, cluttered classrooms and dull decor.
- **An uncomfortable place** with hard chairs and awkward tables, few blinds to keep out the sun, and no quiet rooms.
- **A dangerous environment** with bullies, both amongst fellow learners and staff, to navigate and no-one to talk to about our problems.
- **A non-listening school** with no children on the governing body, no class representatives and no voting for teachers. In

other words, the bully mentality is the official culture of the school.

- **An inflexible school** with rigid timetables, endless exams, compulsory homework, with a one-size-fits-all curriculum.
- **An irrelevant school** where there is little chance to learn through experience, experiments and exploration.
- **A hostile school** where you are treated like empty vessels to be filled with information, where teachers do not treat you as individuals, where children and adults cannot talk freely to each other, and your opinion does not matter.
- **A school operating as a day prison** with a bully atmosphere and ideology: 'You will do it our way – or else'.

Dea Birkett comments: thirty-four years after the first *School that I'd Like*, very few of the suggestions put forward have been acted on. Then the mandate was just under 1000 children's voices. Now it is over 15,000. *"The incredibly huge response to the competition shows that teachers and pupils all over the country realise that the system is outdated, that it does not allow decent expression of the values of creativity and independent thought that are needed in the new post-industrial world,"* said John Clifford, a winner in the original competition. He might have added it remains profoundly anti-democratic and persistently learner-hostile.

* * * * *

Surviving the British school system: a toolbox for change
by Charlie Cooper,

Background

This article builds on the findings of the author's own recent investigation into perspectives on school exclusion, published by Education Now Books as *Understanding School Exclusion: challenging processes of docility* (Cooper, 2002), and feedback on these findings from teachers. It argues that the current education system is causing profound harm to both pupils and teachers, and suggests the need for change built upon a free and open debate involving pupils, teachers and parents/carers. To assist pupils in particular to engage effectively in this debate, this article recommends reviving *The Little Red Schoolbook* (LRSB), originally published in Denmark in 1969 as a guide aimed at showing young people *"ways in which you can influence your own lives"* (Hansen and Jensen, 1971). A revised LRSB would serve as a key text in citizenship education, providing young people with invaluable support for their own personal and political development, as well as a toolbox resource for challenging oppression. However, because *"potentially explosive questions about the nature of British society are sidelined in schools"* (Bamber and Murphy, 1999 p.233), this recommendation will not receive widespread support.

The Little Red Schoolbook

The LRSB was written by Søren Hansen and Jesper Jensen, both schoolteachers in Denmark, as a reference manual for children covering a range of educational issues, including how to challenge the school system. The English translation was published in 1971 and in Britain it became the subject of a 'moral panic'. Secret Home Office papers published in 1999 revealed how the police had singled out the LRSB for prosecution. Detective Chief Inspector George Fenwick, then in charge of the 'dirty squad', justified this by claiming the LRSB was indecent (Travis, 1999). Twenty-six pages on sex education in the original edition were declared obscene by a London magistrate on the grounds that they would *"deprave and corrupt"* young people (Hansen and Jensen, 1971 p.10). 1971 also saw the start of the 'School Kids' Oz case, the longest obscenity trial in British history. The case concerned issue 28 of the magazine, published in May 1970.

This edition devoted a significant amount of space to the work of school pupils, including extracts on sexuality, drugs and the school system (e.g. *"examinations are a primitive method of recording a tiny, often irrelevant, section of the behaviour of an individual under bizarre conditions"*), themes also covered in the LRSB. Of particular concern to the moral guardians of the period was the inclusion of a cartoon of Rupert the Bear, symbol of childhood innocence, seemingly having sex with the American comic character Gipsy Granny. Charges were brought under the 1959 Obscene Publications Act. As the LRSB stated at the time:

> *"In 1885 a law made it illegal to have sexual intercourse with a girl under 16. Although boys and girls become sexually mature much earlier these days, the 'age of consent' for girls*

is still 16. Our laws assume that boys under 14 simply aren't capable of it." (Hansen and Jensen, 1971 p.95)

In Australia, Doug Anthony, deputy PM, described the LRSB as a handbook for *"juvenile revolution and anarchy"*, and said that its *"subversive nature endangered society"* (Stephens, 2003 p.1). In reality, the LRSB is a manual offering children and young people strategies for actively influencing their own life experiences. It is based on the premise that children's and young people's experiences and opinions matter, and are as equally valid as those of adults. It offers children and young people a toolbox for developing the knowledge, skills, attributes and values needed to make informed choices in respect of their education, sexuality and drug use. It promotes the principle that children and young people should have the opportunity to *genuinely* participate in those decision-making processes which substantively affect their lives. Far from being 'subversive', the LRSB advocates that those wanting change should campaign politely within democratic boundaries.

Understanding School Exclusion

On 27 January 2003, I disseminated the findings of my research on school exclusions to teachers at a hotel in a major city. One significant finding of this research was that many pupils *and* teachers held a similar concern that an inclusive education system was not possible under its present structure, largely because it had become too narrowly focused on meaningless managerialist targets - testing, inspections, league tables and so forth. As one teacher argued:

"The growing emphasis on statistics and exam performance seems to be making it ever more difficult to deal with children in ways that are honestly relevant to them. An inclusive system implies to me that every child's needs can be included in so far as every child is placed in his/her best and most appropriate learning environment. This aspect seems to be of increasingly low priority".

Another teacher added that 'individualism' could not be catered for in the mainstream system. *"If someone is having a 'problem', schools don't reach out to understand or help them. They'd rather ignore them or, worse still, banish/exclude them".* He went on: *"This impacts upon all pupils in respect of social/moral values. It does not teach or foster tolerance, caring, kindness or respect for* others. It only emphasises that 'normal', 'averages' and 'sameness' are good. Anything 'other' - different behaviours - should not be tolerated, understood or respected". He felt that education continued to be "élitist, serving to perpetuate existing structures of power". He went on: "Genuine 'inclusion' would bring about such changes in education. We'd produce an environment within which all kinds of things were possible. Time for anger and time for learning. Teachers are not trained for this - not measured for it!"

Of serious concern is the notion that the managerialist agenda governing our education system may be fostering a 'docile' teaching profession, fearful of offering opinions. As one teacher stated: "League tables and performance targets, deeply controlled by the political system, have created a fear to speak out amongst the teaching profession. Even if supported by the union, voicing opinions or criticising can lead to teachers being ostracised. Life is made a misery if you challenge! Because of this, and because of personal and financial commitments, many teachers comply with the system". This teacher was adamant that the education system itself has to change. In particular, he felt, as many teachers do, that the existing performance targets schools are expected to work to should be scrapped: "The current 'New Labour system' does not make it possible properly to develop children's learning and sense of personal significance, values and responsibilities and your book presents this situation lucidly and makes clear the argument for shifting priorities in education".

Teachers and pupils have both become victims of a brutally uniform and authoritarian education system. In response, and as Hansen and Jensen argued over thirty years ago:

> "Teachers and pupils ought to work together for change. There doesn't have to be conflict between them. In fact teachers have as little real power as pupils. They don't decide the content of their own education. They don't decide what to teach. And they decide very little about their own bad conditions of work ... Real changes to the advantage of both teacher and pupils should come from those personally involved." (Hansen and Jensen, 1971 p.206)

One teacher thought the idea of a booklet informing parents/carers and pupils on how to survive the school system would be a good idea – "informed people equals more capable people". Building on this idea, the next section advocates reviving the LRSB and considers how it might look now.

A Little Red Schoolbook for today

A new edition of the LRSB could be framed within the context of the 1989 UN Convention on the Rights of the Child. Article 12 in particular sets out the rights of children in respect of participation:

> "1. Parties shall assure to the child who is capable of forming his or her own views the right to express those views freely in all matters affecting the child, the views of the child being given due weight in accordance with the age and maturity of the child.
>
> "2. For this purpose, the child shall in particular be provided the opportunity to be heard in any judicial and administrative proceedings affecting the child, either directly, or through a representative or an appropriate body, in a manner consistent with the procedural rules of national law."

(Article 12, 1989 UN Convention on the Rights of the Child)

My own research found that such rights are flagrantly ignored within the school system. None of the schools involved in the research allowed pupils the right to express their views on the way the school system operated, never mind giving these views serious consideration. Few schools appear to recognise the potential of children's participation to enrich decision making, or to contribute towards genuine notions of citizenship.

Similar concerns were raised by a group of sixth formers doing Sociology A-level at a private school in Lincolnshire. On 4th April 2003, I facilitated a workshop on school exclusion with this group and they expressed similar feelings about their school experience to those expressed by excluded pupils I had met - particularly the feeling of being 'disrespected' by teachers. Moreover, in my school exclusion research, pupils (and parents/carers) felt that they were given inadequate opportunity to be heard when the decision to exclude was made. This raises serious questions about the consistency of such processes in terms of legal and social justice.

A key principle behind Article 12 is that teachers are no longer expected to be mere providers of education, but to facilitate learning through more dialogical processes designed to empower children to have an influence over both their own learning, and their personal and social development. This is spelt out more in Article 29:

> "*1. Parties agree that the education of the child shall be directed to:*
> *(a) The development of the child's personality, talents and mental and physical abilities to their fullest potential;*
> *(b) The development of respect for human rights and fundamental freedoms, and for the principles enshrined in the Charter of the United Nations;*
> *(c) The development of respect for the child's parents, his or her own cultural identity, language and values, for the national values of the country in which the child is living, the country from which he or she may originate, and for civilizations different from his or her own;*
> *(d) The preparation of the child for responsible life in a free society, in the spirit of understanding, peace, tolerance, equality of sexes, and friendship among all peoples, ethnic, national and religious groups and persons of indigenous origin;*
> *(e) The development of respect for the natural environment."*
> (Article 29, 1989 UN Convention on the Rights of the Child)

As described by teachers above, schools do not offer all children the opportunity to develop their talents and abilities to their fullest potential, or foster tolerance and respect. Education's narrow focus on testing is suffocating potential and innovation. As Hansen and Jensen argued back in 1969:

> *"Schools often use exams and tests to frighten you into working ... By far the greatest number of exams don't show what you know ... They may show what you've learnt parrot-fashion or had knocked into you. They rarely show whether you think for yourself and find things out for yourself ... In schools which have a lot of school exams and tests, education suffers. You don't learn about the subjects themselves: you learn how to cope with tests and exams. **This can be changed.**"*
> (Hansen and Jensen, 1971 pp.162-163, original emphasis).

As one teacher in my own study argues (see above), by fostering uniformity and conformity schools fail to nurture understanding, tolerance and respect for 'difference'. This clearly causes greater harm than good, a situation that needs to be challenged.

The original LRSB contains a wealth of information on challenging oppression - how to have an influence; how to make a complaint; how to demand one's rights; coping with the British school system; forms of representation; understanding the role of education for society. Much of this material is still pertinent today; perhaps more so in view of education's narrow focus on labour-market needs and social conformity. At the same time, new material drawing on more recent discussions on the possibilities for critical practice could be included in an updated LRSB. Drawing on the ideas of Bamber and Murphy, I recently ran a workshop with a group of youth workers at the University of Hull on the possibilities for critical practice in education (with a particular focus on school exclusions).

Bamber and Murphy stress education's potential for creating a fairer and more cohesive society. In particular, they see a role for education in raising awareness about key concepts of power and forms of social action connecting the personal to the political. They argue the need to uncover and question the basic assumptions upon which power holders exert their control and allow deep social injustices to remain. For Bamber and Murphy: *"Critical practice is not an event, a final or ultimate moment of radical work, but a process of working towards a preferred anti-oppressive future"* (Bamber and Murphy, 1999 p.227). Basically, this process involves working with groups through three stages:

- Stage One - developing a group's understanding of the nature of 'the problem' (based on experience or one's reading) and how they personally feel about it.
- Stage Two - negotiating with the group to find a consensus position on the nature of the problem, and that something ought to be done about it.
- Stage Three - negotiating with the group to find a consensus on what exactly should be done and agreeing how to go about this.

Working with groups of young people in this way, they become *"sites of democratic activity in which young people attempt to address issues of social justice in a rational manner"* (Bamber and Murphy, 1999 p.241). Working through the three stages myself with the youth-work students at Hull, the following issues emerged:

Stage One - the nature of school exclusions

- Lack of parental support/responsibility/role models?

- Teachers pressurised/frustrated (lack of resources/freedoms/rigid system)?
- Excluded pupils abandoned/difficult to reintegrate?
- Stigmatization/labelling of children?
- Lack of flexibility within the curriculum (to tailor it to individual pupils/focus on the academic)?
- Underlying causes of challenging behaviour ignored (being in care/family problems)?
- Culture of education system (inflexible/uniform hierarchical/managerialist/unaccountable/competition between schools)?
- Learning difficulties (dyslexia/dyspraxia)?

Most students felt that exclusion was not an answer, although some were ambivalent (what about the bullies?). The majority thought more could be done to help young people, and blamed the politicians for not doing enough.

Stage Two - consensus on the key issues

- Structural problems (social, political, economic - e.g. poverty, unequal power relationships, race, class and gender, etc.)
- The managerialist school system (e.g. competition, PRP, league tables, performance targets, national curriculum, OFSTED inspections, lack of time/resources)
- Individual factors (e.g. family breakdown, no discipline, no positive role models, learning difficulties).

There was a consensus that these issues should be dealt with.

Stage Three - what should be done?

- Multi-dimensional approach
- Flexible curriculum and assessment
- Ask young people what they want
- Devolve more power and resources to teachers
- Informal education - a flexible, negotiated curriculum.

Due to lack of time, the students did not develop ideas on how exactly they would effect change. Despite this, the majority did find that this three-stage process offered a valuable tool for developing ideas on anti-oppressive practice. Consequently, such a model could prove a valuable reference source in an updated LRSB.

Conclusion

The current education system is a cause of harm to pupils and teachers. To assist pupils in particular to resist education's oppressive practices, this article calls for the revival of the LRSB to serve citizenship education, and provide young people with support for their own personal and political development. An updated edition of the LRSB would also act, as it did back in the 1970s, as a toolbox resource for challenging oppressive practices. However, because of its radical potential, it is unlikely that such a suggestion would receive widespread support from within the British education system.

References:

Bamber, J. and Murphy, H. (1999), 'Youth Work: The Possibilities for Critical Practice', *Journal of Youth Studies*, 2:2, pp.227-242.

Cooper, C. (2002), *Understanding School Exclusion: challenging processes of docility*, Nottingham: Education Now Books/The University of Hull.

Hansen, S. and Jensen, J. (1971), *The Little Red Schoolbook*, London: stage 1.

Stephens, T. (2003), 'Release of "subversive" book marks new moral chapter', *The Sydney Morning Herald*, 1 January.

Travis, A. (1999), 'Oz trial lifted lid on porn squad bribery', *Guardian Unlimited website*, 13 November.

Postscripts

Whatever you do to it, it's still a school
A boy who had just left school was asked by his former headmaster what he thought of the splendid new buildings. *"It could be all marble"*, he replied, *"but it would still be a bloody school"*.

Newsom Report 1963

The odds are all on the house's side ...
"School is like roulette or something. You can't just ask: Well, what's the point of it? The point of it is to do it, to get through and into college. But you have to figure out the system or you can't win, because the odds are all on the house's side."

Student in The Experience of Schooling, ed. M. Silberman, p.324

Part three:

Learn your lines, or, stay a victim of compulsory mis-education

by Roland Meighan

Those representing the vested interests of the mass, coercive learning system known as schools, have learnt their lines in government controlled teacher-training institutions, from a non-radical mass media or the market-place of service providers. Anyone wanting to deal with damage limitation needs to learn another script and below are some quotations I have selected that should help. Learn some of them so that you can repeat them at will!

"Schools have transformed learning from one of the most rewarding of all human activities into a painful, boring, dull, fragmenting, mind-shrinking, soul-shrivelling experience."
E. T. Hall

"One answer to the question *'What is wrong with schools?'* is **291**. This was the number of discrete criticisms Nigel Wright indexed in his research on radical ideas in education – and that was before the re-invention of the National Curriculum, the obscenity of School League Tables and all the other apparatus of the return to regressive schooling, from 1988 onwards."
Roland Meighan

"For all the children some of the time, and for some of the children all of the time, the classroom resembles a cage from which there is no escape."
Philip Jackson

"No teacher ever said: *'Don't value uncertainty and tentativeness, don't question questions, above all don't think!'* The message is communicated quietly, insidiously, relentlessly and efficiently through the structure of the classroom: through the role of the teacher, the role of the student, ... the 'doings' that are praised or censured."
Neil Postman and Charles Weingartner

"Much of our expenditure on teachers and plant is wasted by attempting to teach people what they do not want to learn in a situation that they would rather not be involved in." *Colin Ward*

"Schools have not necessarily much to do with education ... they are mainly institutions of control where certain basic habits must be instilled in the young. Education is quite different and has little place in school." *Winston Churchill*

"It's not that I feel that school is a good idea gone wrong, but a wrong idea from the word go. It's a nutty notion that we can have a place where nothing but learning happens, cut off from the rest of life." *John Holt*

"It is not possible to spend any prolonged period visiting public school classrooms without being appalled by the mutilation visible everywhere - mutilation of spontaneity, of joy in learning, or pleasure in creating, or sense of self ... Because adults take the schools so much for granted, they fail to appreciate what grim, joyless places most American schools are (they are much the same in most countries), how oppressive and petty are the rules by which they are governed, how intellectually sterile and aesthetically barren the atmosphere, what an appalling lack of civility obtains on the part of teachers and principals, what contempt they unconsciously display for students as students." *Charles Silberman*

"Trying to get more learning out of the current system is like trying to get the Pony Express to compete with the telegraph by breeding faster ponies." *Edward Fiske*

"Education is not the filling of a pail, but the lighting of a fire."
W. B. Yeats

"Is a damage limitation policy really necessary? And does every parent using schools need one? John Stuart Mill in *On Liberty* (1859, p.177) observed that:

> *'A general State Education is a mere contrivance for moulding people to be exactly like one another, and as the mould in which it casts them is that which pleases the dominant power in the government, whether this be a monarchy, an aristocracy, or a majority of the existing generation ... it establishes a despotism over the mind, leading by a natural tendency to one over the body.'*

This seems to me to be (a) just as true now as in 1859 and just as anti-democratic, and (b) just the opposite of an 'organic, toxin-free learning' outcome." *Roland Meighan*

"A majority want the schools to be even more rigid, threatening, and punitive than they are, and they will probably become so."
John Holt

"In the 20th century, provision has come before clients. You designed the courses and then tried to find some students to fill them. It is the other way round in the future: find the clients, find out what they want and need and then design (or redesign) your provision." *Sir Christopher Ball*

"We are faced with the paradoxical fact that education has become one of the chief obstacles to intelligence and freedom of thought."
Bertrand Russell

"The case for traditional education seems to me to be much weaker than it has been, and is getting ever weaker, and the case for an education which will give a child primarily not knowledge and certainty but resourcefulness, flexibility, curiosity, skill in learning, readiness to unlearn - the case grows ever stronger." *John Holt*

"The problems of mass, coercive schooling are that, (a) it is mass not personalised, (b) it is coercive not invitational, and (c) it is schooling not education." *Roland Meighan*

"From my earliest memories of school (going back some 60 years) right up to the present, I am struck by how recurrent are the standard complaints and how little things change. Students are still locked into classrooms, still chained to desks, still herded through lessons that are far from reality and cruelly indifferent to individual differences in brains, background, talent and feelings."
Gene Lehman

"We may get our way but we don't get their learning. They may have to comply but they won't change. We have pushed out their goals with ours and stolen their purposes. It is a pernicious form of theft which kills off the will to learn." *Charles Handy*

"Some true educational experiences are bound to occur in schools. They occur, however, despite and not because of school."
Everett Reimer

"My schooling not only failed to teach me what it professed to be teaching, but prevented me from being educated to an extent which infuriates me when I think of all I might have learned at home by myself." *George Bernard Shaw*

"In nine schools out of ten, on nine days out of ten, in nine lessons out of ten, the teacher is engaged in laying thin films of information on the surface of the child's mind and then after a brief interval he is skimming these off in order to satisfy himself that they have been duly laid."
Edmond Holmes. (Chief Inspector of Schools, 1910, who spent 30 years trying to make the first UK National Curriculum work.)

"School is the Army for kids. Adults make them go there, and when they get there, adults tell them what to do, bribe and threaten them into doing it, and punish them when they don't." *John Holt*

"Students do not participate in choosing the goals, the curriculum, or the manner of working. These things are chosen for the students. Students have no part in the choice of teaching personnel, nor any voice in educational policy. Likewise the teachers often have no choice in choosing their administrative officers ... All this is in striking contrast to all the teaching about the virtues of democracy, the importance of the 'free world,' and the like. The political practices of the school stand in the most striking contrast to what is taught. While being taught that freedom and responsibility are the glorious features of our democracy, students are experiencing powerlessness, and having almost no opportunity to exercise choice or carry responsibility." *Carl Rogers*

"I was an A-level junkie" writes Giles Foden in the *Guardian* 22/8/95 (he sat and got six) "All those grades. Could A stand for alienation, B for boredom and C for control?" he asks.

"They work to pass, not to know: and outraged science takes her revenge. They do pass and they don't know." *Thomas Huxley*

"Nobody grew taller by being measured." *Philip Gammage*

"It is the great triumph of compulsory government monopoly mass schooling that among even the best of my fellow teachers, and among even the best of my students' parents, only a small number can imagine a different way to do things." *John Taylor Gatto*

"What we want to see is the child in pursuit of knowledge, and not knowledge in pursuit of the child."   *George Bernard Shaw*

"When I was teaching in school, a man came to a parents' meeting and complained about the extraordinary amount of testing we were doing. His words went right to the heart of the matter: 'You're like a gardener who constantly pulls his plants up by the roots to see if they're growing'."   *John Holt*

"We can no more ordain learning by order, coercion and commandment than we can produce love by rape or threat."
Peter Jones

"American kids like watching violence on TV and in the movies because violence is being done to them, both at school and at home. It builds up a tremendous amount of anger ... The problem is not violence on TV. That's a symptom ... The real problem is the violence of anti-life, unaffectionate, and punitive homes, and disempowering, deadening compulsory schooling, all presented with an uncomprehending smile."   *Jerry Mintz*

"The prevention of free inquiry is unavoidable so long as the purpose of education is to produce belief rather than thought, to compel the young to hold positive opinions on doubtful matters rather than let them see the doubtfulness and be encouraged to independence of mind. Education ought to foster the wish for the truth, not the conviction that some particular creed is the truth."
Bertrand Russell

"Thousands of caring, humane people work in schools, as teachers, and aides and administrators, but the abstract logic of the institution overwhelms their individual contributions. Although teachers do care and do work very, very hard, the institution is psychopathic; it has no conscience. It rings a bell and the young man in the middle of writing a poem must close his notebook and move to a different cell ... "   *John Taylor Gatto*

"There is nothing on earth intended for innocent people so horrible as a school. To begin with, it is a prison. But in some respects more cruel than a prison. In a prison, for instance, you are not forced to read books written by the prison warders and the governor."   *George Bernard Shaw*

"There must be in the world many parents who, like the present author, have young children whom they are anxious to educate as well as possible, but reluctant to expose to the evils of existing educational institutions."
Bertrand Russell

"The schools this country needs today must be institutions which abandon any and all attempts to limit the free pursuit of knowledge that every child, and every adult, engages in naturally, without any outside goading."
Daniel Greenberg

"The spontaneous wish to learn, which every normal child possesses, as shown in its efforts to walk and talk, should be the driving force in education."
Bertrand Russell

"To learn to know oneself, and to find a life worth living and work worth doing, is problem and challenge enough, without having to waste time on the fake and unworthy challenges of school - pleasing the teacher, staying out of trouble, fitting in with the gang, being popular, doing what everyone else does."
John Holt

"Most criticism of the old education, and the old concepts it conserves and transmits, from Paul Goodman to John Gardner, makes the point that the students who endure it come out as passive, acquiescent, dogmatic, intolerant, authoritarian, inflexible, conservative personalities who desperately need to resist change in an effort to keep their illusion of certainty intact."
Neil Postman and Charles Weingartner

"The new education has as its purpose the development of a new kind of person, one who - as a result of internalising a different set of concepts - is an active, inquiring, flexible, creative, innovative, tolerant, liberal personality, who can face uncertainty and ambiguity without disorientation, who can formulate viable new meanings to meet changes in the environment which threaten individual and mutual survival.

"The new education, in sum, is new because it consists of having students use the concepts most appropriate to the world in which we all must live. All of these concepts constitute the dynamics of the question-questioning, meaning-making process that can be called 'learning how to learn'."
Neil Postman and Charles Weingartner

"If personal quality is to be preserved, definite teaching must be reduced to a minimum, and criticism must never be carried to such lengths as to produce timidity in self-expression. But these maxims are not likely to lead to work that will be pleasing to an inspector."
Bertrand Russell

"Using school as a sorting mechanism, we appear to be on the way to creating a caste system, complete with untouchables who wander through subway trains begging and who sleep upon the streets."
John Taylor Gatto

"My grandmother wanted me to have an education so she kept me out of school." *Margaret Mead*

"The only real object of education is to leave a man in the condition of continually asking questions." *Tolstoy*

"People must be educated once more to know their place."
UK Department of Education official responsible for National Curriculum planning

"A school, like a fascist state, is about the business of compelling people to conform to a pattern of behaviour and a way of thinking decided by the few who hold power over them." *Chris Shute*

"Fundamentally, there is no right education except growing up into a worthwhile world. Indeed, our excessive concern with problems of education at present simply means that the grown-ups do not have such a world." *Paul Goodman*

"Either what is offered for learning must be experienced by the adolescents as illuminating, as informing their own life purposes, or it will be, at best, tolerated, and at worst, rejected." *James Hemming*

"School is necessary to produce the habits and expectations of the managed consumer society." *Ivan Illich*

"When we put together in one scheme such elements as a prescribed curriculum, similar assignments for all students, lecturing as almost the only mode of instruction, standard texts by which all students are externally evaluated, and instructor-chosen grades as the measure of learning, then we can almost guarantee that meaningful learning will be at an absolute minimum." *Carl Rogers*

"Assessment, more than religion, has become the opiate of the people." *Patricia Broadfoot*

"The disappearance of a sense of responsibility is the most far-reaching consequence of submission to authority." *Stanley Milgram*

"School has become the replacement for church in our secular society, and like church it requires that its teachings must be taken on faith." *John Taylor Gatto*

"I have never allowed schooling to interfere with my education." *Mark Twain*

"Education with inert ideas is not only useless; it is above all things harmful." *Alfred North Whitehead*

"It follows logically from the banking notion of consciousness that the educator's role is to regulate the way the world 'enters into' the students. His task is to organise a process which already happens spontaneously, to 'fill' the students by making deposits of information which he considers constitute true knowledge. And since men 'receive' the world as passive entities, education should make them more passive still, and adapt them to the world. The educated man is the adapted man, because he is more 'fit' for the world. Translated into practice, this concept is well suited to the purpose of the oppressors, whose tranquillity rests on how well men fit the world the oppressors have created, and how little they question it." *Paulo Friere*

"The hard task of education is to liberate and strengthen a youth's initiative and at the same time to see to it that he knows what is necessary to cope with the ongoing activities and culture of society, so that his initiative can be relevant. It is absurd to think that this task can be accomplished by so much sitting in a box facing front, manipulating symbols at the direction of distant administrators. This is rather a way to regiment and brainwash." *Paul Goodman*

"It is an iron law of education that rigid systems produce rigid people, and flexible systems produce flexible people." *Roland Meighan*

"People who can't think are ripe for dictatorships." *Carl Rogers*

"It is absurd and anti-life to move from cell to cell at the sound of a gong for every day of your natural youth in an institution that allows you no privacy and even follows you into the sanctuary of your home demanding that you do its 'homework'."
John Taylor Gatto

"What good fortune for those in power that people do not think."
Adolf Hitler

"If a curriculum is to be effective ... it must contain different ways of activating children, different ways of presenting sequences, different opportunities ... A curriculum, in short, must contain many tracks leading to the same general goal."
Jerome Bruner

"I deeply believe that traditional teaching is an almost completely futile, wasteful, overrated function in today's changing world. It is successful mostly in giving children who can't grasp the material, a sense of failure."
Carl Rogers

"The wish to preserve the past rather than the hope of creating the future dominates the minds of those who control the teaching of the young."
Bertrand Russell

"True education does not quiet things down, it stirs them up. It awakens consciousness. It destroys myth. It empowers people."
John Holt

"Education ... has produced a vast population able to read but unable to distinguish what is worth reading."
George Macauley Trevelyan

"Happiness in childhood is absolutely necessary to the production of the best type of human being."
Bertrand Russell

"That children do not come to school by choice is another terrible indictment of our whole educational system."
John Kirkbride

"There is no point ... in learning the 'answers' for very soon there will be different answers."
Paul Goodman

"A boy will toil uphill with a toboggan for the sake of a few brief moments of bliss during the descent; no one has to urge him to be industrious, and however he may puff and pant he is still happy."
Bertrand Russell

"All my own work as a teacher and learner has led me to believe ... that teaching is a very strong medicine, which like all strong medicines can quickly and easily turn into a poison. At the right time (i.e. when the student has asked for it) and in very small doses, it can indeed help learning. But at the wrong times, or in too large doses, it will slow down learning or prevent it altogether." *John Holt*

"I remember spending the greater part of my childhood wondering about adults. Were they ever children? From their behaviour toward children it seemed to me quite clearly that they could never have possibly been children." *Ashley Montague*

"I owe more to my ability to fantasise than to any knowledge I've ever acquired." *Albert Einstein*

"Whilst my photocopying was being completed I saw a notice on the wall of the Kall Kwik Print shop. It said: *'Customised: we listen, we understand, we find the solution that's right for you'*. I thought this would make a splendid slogan for the next learning system to replace the present learning system of compulsory, coercive schooling followed by the dreary steeplechase of university courses. Its slogan appears to be: *'Standardised: you listen, we only understand coercion and dominance, you accept the solution we decide'*. The slogan in the shop, on the other hand, assumes that people deserve a personalised service, not a standardised one." *Roland Meighan*

"Children who are lectured to, learn how to lecture; if they are admonished, they learn how to admonish; if scolded, they learn how to scold; if ridiculed, they learn how to ridicule; if humiliated, they learn how to humiliate; if their psyche is killed, they will learn how to kill - the only question is who will be killed: oneself, others or both." *Alice Miller*

"What the world now needs is not competition but organisation and co-operation; all belief in the utility of competition has become an anachronism. ... the emotions connected with it are the emotions of hostility and ruthlessness. The conception of society as an organic whole is very difficult for those whose minds have been steeped in competitive ideas. Ethically, therefore, no less than economically, it is undesirable to teach the young to be competitive."
Bertrand Russell

"They know enough who know how to learn." *Henry Adams*

"It is very difficult for people to believe the simple fact that *every persecutor was once a victim*. Yet it should be very obvious that someone who was allowed to feel free and strong from childhood does not have the need to humiliate another person." *Alice Miller*

"What we can learn best from good teachers is how to teach ourselves better." *John Holt*

"When I look back at all the crap I learned in high school, it's a wonder I can think at all." *Paul Simon*

"Schools learned long ago that the way to keep children from thinking is to keep them busy." *Everett Reimer*

"It is in fact nothing short of a miracle that the modern methods of instruction have not entirely strangled the holy curiosity of inquiry; for this delicate little plant, aside from stimulation, stands mainly in need of freedom; without this it goes to wrack and ruin without fail." *Albert Einstein*

"... the school institution 'schools' very well, though it does not 'educate'; that's inherent in the design of the thing. It's not the fault of bad teachers or too little money spent. It's just impossible for education and schooling ever to be the same thing."
John Taylor Gatto

"We need to scrap schools and replace them with something more educational. Schools are (a) obsolete in what is now an information rich society, (b) counter-productive in producing the wrong kind of person with the wrong habits, (c) an abuse of three and sometimes four basic human rights." *Roland Meighan*

"One head teacher told John's parents to make his home life less interesting so that he would not be so bored at school."
in Times Educational Supplement, 20/9/96, Features, p.3

Final thoughts:

"Deep in my bones I remain convinced that ultimately it will be the deschoolers who are proved right, and that far in the future our descendants will view the whole concept of the school with mirth and disbelief." *Gerald Haigh*

"*'We are just miserable rule-followers ...'*. This is the verdict of a teacher in South Africa, reported by Clive Harber in *State of Transition*, London: Symposium Books, 2001. But it could be anywhere in the world, given Edward de Bono's verdict that **all the schooling systems he has encountered in the world are a disgrace**. I have to agree, for all the ones I have encountered are also a disgrace, although some are larger disasters and some are smaller ones. Only a few are trying to be more democratic and are generally less constipated in their approach, having a just a few echoes of natural learning. Not surprisingly, the *'miserable rule-followers'* are currently leaving teaching in droves and in disgust, and many who stay explain that they would leave if they could."

Roland Meighan

"When you take the free will out of education, that turns it into schooling." *John Taylor Gatto*

"I believe that the computer presence will enable us to so modify the learning environment outside the classroom that much, if not all, the knowledge schools presently try to teach with such pain and expense and such limited success will be learned, as the child learns to walk, painlessly, successfully, and without organised instruction. This obviously implies that schools, as we know them today, will have no place in the future. But it is an open question whether they will adapt by transforming themselves into something new or whither away and be replaced."

Seymour Papert

"It used to worry me that, as a teacher, I was engaged in what was essentially microscopic fascism." *Chris Shute*

"Whatever crushes individuality is despotism, by whatever name it be called." *John Stuart Mill*

"School is a twelve-year jail sentence where bad habits are the only curriculum truly learned. I teach school and win awards doing it. I should know." *John Taylor Gatto*

"In examinations the foolish ask questions that the wise cannot answer." *Oscar Wilde*

"Shakespeare did not write with a view to boring schoolchildren; he wrote with a view to delighting his audiences. If he does not give you delight, you had better ignore him." *Bertrand Russell*

"The authority of those who teach is very often a hindrance to those who wish to learn."
Cicero

"Break their wills betimes; begin this great work before they can run alone, before they can speak plain, or perhaps speak at all. Let him have nothing he cries for, absolutely nothing, great or small. Make him do as he is bid, if you whip him ten times running to effect it. Break his will now and his soul will live, and he will bless you to all eternity."
John Wesley

"The education of today is nothing more than drill ... children must become accustomed to obey, to believe, to think according to the social dogmas which govern us."
Francisco Ferrer

"Nothing in education is so astonishing as the amount of ignorance it accumulates in the form of inert facts."
Henry Adams

"The skilled teacher, when a pupil is entrusted to his care, will first of all seek to discover his ability and natural disposition and will next observe how the mind of his pupil is to be handled ... for in this respect there is an unbelievable variety, and types of mind are no less numerous than types of body."
Quintillian

"All sorts of intellectual systems - Christianity, Socialism, Patriotism etc., - are ready, like orphan asylums, to give safety in return for servitude. A free mental life cannot be as warm and comfortable and sociable as a life enveloped in a creed."
Bertrand Russell

"Among all the leading figures of the Third Reich, I have not been able to find a single one who did not have a strict and rigid upbringing. Shouldn't that give us a great deal of food for thought?"
Alice Miller

"... there can be no agreement between those who regard education as a means of instilling certain definite beliefs, and those who think that it should produce the power of independent judgement."
Bertrand Russell

"Meanwhile, education - compulsory schooling, compulsory learning - is a tyranny and a crime against the human mind and spirit. Let all those escape it who can, any way they can."
John Holt

Part four:

The point of view of the parents

My attempts to survive the system

by Jane Dent
(First published in *Choice in Education* 56, Nov 2002)

1. Look for the good things

My first child, Otto, went to school for 12 years so I saw the good and bad of the school system. Actually, there was only one good thing about it and that was the 6 hours free childminding I got every day (good for me anyway). I saw a lot of bad, but the main things that mattered to me, and still matter, were lack of respect for children, lack of kindness, and the many incidents of injustice that I witnessed. It makes no logical sense that children should be considered LESS sensitive than adults, yet schools (and most parents, sadly) operate on this assumption. It is considered OK to humiliate a 5-year-old in front of 30 other people, but how would we adults feel if it happened to us?

Personally, I would feel devastated for days, yet children are expected to shrug it off, and if they do not, well, they are 'sulking', which is further cause for public humiliation. And we wonder why, when they are big enough and articulate enough, children rebel. Society blames it on their hormones. Looks to me like they are getting their own back, making themselves heard at last. Seems fair enough to me ...

Anyway, back to the subject. Although I joined *Education Otherwise* (EO) when Otto was 4, home education seemed very scary. So many home educators seemed to me to be such saintly and self-sacrificing people, completely focused on their children. This was the impression I was getting from EO newsletters, plus I had met a home educator who was very nice but also fitted this description. I did not think I could be like that; it would be like giving up my own life. I get bored playing with children.

2. Con yourself – 'this one is better than the rest'

So, school it was. I persuaded myself, as so many parents do, that the school I had found for him was better than the rest. But over the years, I realised that no matter what a school said about itself at its open day, your child's well being, or otherwise, depended mainly on the personality of the adult whose care they were in, i.e. their teacher for that year.

3. Make a grand gesture - then retreat

Being a hot-headed person, I occasionally made the grand gesture of marching out of the school dragging Otto behind me, on account of some injustice I had witnessed (not to my own child; they never treat your child badly in front of you). But then, after a couple of days attempting the 'kitchen table' style of home education and losing my temper with Otto a lot along the way, I would decide I was probably going to do more damage to him than the school and I would take poor Otto back with my tail between my legs.

4. Tell a teacher the truth – and later apologise

I remember one occasion in Otto's classroom, when a four-year-old boy proudly showed the teaching assistant the Lego house he had made (back in the days when children were allowed to play in school). To my amazement, she violently smashed the house to pieces in front of him, shouting furiously, *"THIS IS NOT A HOUSE YOU LAZY BOY! HOUSES HAVE ROOFS"*. I in turn went berserk with her, announced that no son of mine was going to remain in such an environment and marched out of the school with Otto. After a couple of hours at the kitchen table, head in hands, despairing at the thought of being a full-time single parent again, I slunk back into the classroom, swallowed my pride and apologised for shouting at her in front of the class. *"That's all right"*, she said kindly, *"I could tell you weren't feeling well"*.

I wish 1 had known then what I know now: that children learn *anyway* (without the kitchen table scenario), and that home education is such good *fun*, even for us mothers. Best of all, I have also found it can be done with very little **self-sacrifice**. I really wish more people realised that because then more people might do it.

5. Shop around?

When Bobby came along I was in a stable relationship and felt confident enough to try home education if that was what he wanted. He wanted to try nursery though. The first nursery he tried was a bleak place, run by cynical, unhappy adults who, I noticed, would even lie to the children to get them to do what they wanted them to. I stayed with him there every day, and one day I added up the time the children spent sitting quietly 'on their bottoms'. It was one and a quarter hours out of a two and a half hour session. It took me a couple of mornings to decide this was not a good place for young children, that no-one here was on their side. It took Bobby a week. I still feel satisfaction that I was able to tell the teachers (politely this time, but in full detail) exactly what I thought was wrong with the place, including the lying.

But Bobby did not want to give up on the idea of nursery. He wanted to try another one, so we did. This was a much kinder place, and I think Bobby might have stayed for longer, but the headteacher of the school it was attached to would not let Bobby have a part-time place because he was four and, well, *"rules are rules"*. I argued and she bent slightly. She said he could go part-time for the first week, then full-time. Bobby let me leave him on his first (and last!) full day. I came home and cried a bit, then did a dance of freedom round the kitchen, then sat down to PLAN MY FUTURE CAREER. My fantasy of myself as a rich, successful Shirley Conran superwoman-type person was short-lived however. When I picked him up at 3.30, he announced indignantly that he was never going back there. Too much time 'on his bottom' again. Nurseries love that phrase do they not?

So home education it was. Around this time, I was going to a playgroup run by Barry. I told him that I had decided to home educate Bobby, but was feeling isolated from my circle of friends who had put their children in nurseries. Well, not only did Barry reveal that he was a home educator himself, but also that his partner ran a home education group nearby. The next day I went there. I immediately felt completely welcome and at home and have been going there ever since. It was the first time in my life I had been surrounded by so many like-minded people. Four years on, we still go there every week. I do not know who enjoys it more, Bobby or me. I do not know about him, but like to think it has taught *me* how to socialise, which, strangely, seven years at the 25th best school in this country (see 2002 secondary school league tables) did not.

Damage limitation or damage repair?

by Kim Evans

School does not only impinge on school hours. Homework takes out hours available for 'damage limitation' work. There are books to be read, spellings to be practised, maths to be checked, projects to be investigated - sometimes with only a few hours' notice. ('Go to the Library in town tonight and ...' is not an unusual command, even for children too young to get there without adult help.) Schools even send home worksheets for parents to complete with their children, apparently on the basis that all parents need help with basic skills and have to be forced into learning with their children.

Sure, you can limit the damage by explaining to your children what it is that you do not value about school work, with discussions of individuality, equality, rights and choices, but it is the children who have to face the wrath, sarcasm or other punishments of the teacher the next day if it is not done.

To build self-esteem in a child who is getting very different messages from home and school is an extremely difficult task. As an example, when my ten-year-old was trying to learn a piece of music for a school concert, the teacher insisted on her playing what I knew to be a wrong note (b natural instead of b flat) - she just did not know who to believe or which note to play. I challenged the school with a short note to the teacher pointing out the error as tactfully as possible with the result that the teacher gave up rehearsing the piece and awarded an 'effort stamp' to the other child involved who had not disagreed with her judgement! It took a lot of work to restore my child's belief in her ability to play music after this incident - this becomes damage repair, not damage limitation.

Sometimes the teachers' own actions demonstrate much more eloquently than my words how pointless their rules and requirements are. The teacher who insists that each boy has to be separated by at least three girls - in a class of 9 boys and 21 girls, or the one who criticises a whole class for not learning their spelling lists when she has taken away from them for marking the books those spellings were written in, both serve very well to highlight the futility of it all.

Damage limitation was not previously a term that I had consciously considered. I wanted us to *be* a family - something I am very conscious of resenting school-time taking away from us. What is important is that we want to do whatever we do, there are no orders and no pressure (and definitely no worksheets) and the emphasis is on choices and enjoyment. Our activities are in one respect 'business as usual', a natural extension of pre-school activities, but they become real family learning events – I had never heard of a turnstone until recently, for example (and I am learning to resist the temptation to assume that others do not know and need my instruction!). Most of our activities could be 'fitted' to curriculum subjects if we wanted to. We do not usually, but sometimes choose to, just to prove that we are learning, and in a much more interesting way.

In a very important respect, our activities have one big difference from other families doing the same things, where intense pressure is put on the children by their parents to 'succeed' in some way. I see four- and five-year-olds falling off bikes from which parents have removed stabilisers on the grounds that children are too old for such baby things - my children still enjoy riding their first bikes, looking rather like clowns, although they do have their 'grown up' ones as well - I have no wish to hurry their childhoods away. My eight-year-old by her own choice took piano lessons and recently her first piano exam. All three choose to take swimming lessons, but they decide whether or not to take distance badges. I am happy that they are learning to choose how to enjoy themselves. Other parents continually ask how soon the children will be doing the next grade, the next distance badge, and seem to be forever pushing their children to get on, go faster, be better than everyone else. Their children take piano lessons because they (the adults) 'really wanted their children to be able to play the piano'. Why? Where are the children's voices in all this? It seems clear that the idea of doing things for fun, when children and adults are ready and willing, and with more or less equality between adults and children, which seems natural in my family is quite alien to others.

Perhaps that is the secret of damage limitation: it is an act of democracy, not 'spoiling children by giving them everything they want'. Instead, it is giving them an equal voice in the choices and decisions of here and now living, not the vague promise of a 'maybe' voice at some time in the future, to be earned if in the meantime they learn to be dependent on the narrow world of school.

It is a sad reflection on the state of democracy that there are personal costs as well as benefits in trying to have a family life. I am told I 'should' send my children to *Breakfast* and *After School Clubs* so I can get a job that pays more money, and I am considered 'odd' and even 'feckless' for not being prepared to do so, especially when one effect is a long list of 'can't affords'. To do so would mean losing the togetherness and opportunity for talk that our family meals entail, to say nothing of the unhealthy nature of the fatty, sugary food provided at these Clubs. There would be even less time for all the activities we cherish and which limit the damage of school, and yet we are told it 'would not matter' if we had to give up all those things which at heart make us a family.

Next, my role as classroom assistant

I see four-year-olds spending most of their time either sitting on the floor at the teacher's feet, quietly taking in her words, or completing worksheets. The child who needs to be active and the one who wants to tell you what she/he thinks are 'naughty' and punished, sometimes by losing previously earned reward stars or other public humiliation in front of the class. I have gone home and cried sometimes when I have seen this happen. Children who are still learning how to hold a pencil, or how to correctly form letters or numbers have their efforts rubbed out before their eyes and told to do it again. And, yes, I have heard a teacher shouting at five-year-olds demanding to know why they were late for school and telling them they must make sure it does not happen again. How many five-year-olds have responsibility for getting themselves to school on time – or can even tell the time for that matter? And how many parents realise that much of the work on craft items brought home has actually been done by the adults and not by the children?

As a mere assistant in all this, I am as much a prisoner as the children are – neither of us can escape the system or change it, so what can I do? I try to make a difference in lots of small ways. I can talk to the children as equals and join in their play if they want me to. If behaviour needs to be checked for the sake of others or to protect against damage I can talk directly but privately with the child concerned. I can use explanation and reason, not threats.

My sessions are probably noisier than most teachers seem to want, but what of it – I can shut the door. And I can find ways to allow the children choices in what to do. We can make time by going more quickly through what the teacher has set. I can find ways to help them succeed when children are finding set tasks too impossibly difficult. Or we can do what the teacher has set but surround it with plenty of talk, not necessarily 'on task' talk. Or I can cut a few corners or go over time so that the children can complete craft activities for themselves.

By giving myself, my listening, my time, my talk, and respecting their individuality and abilities I try to restore to the children a little control and freedom over their actions – and with it the possibility of confidence and self-esteem. It equates to how I would want my own children to be treated by their teachers (while recognising that they probably are not). I am not so much the spy within as the heretic within. Given the fluid nature of schools where classes change in composition regularly I will probably never know if I have succeeded. I do still find myself wondering about the fates of the first children I worked with like this nearly 25 years ago. I can see no reason, pressures of National Curriculum notwithstanding, why teachers should not also treat children as human beings of equal worth. That is surely a fundamental human right?

Identifying the problem

"Education as it has come to be practiced in our society is the destruction of the child. Born into curiosity and driven by the innate need to learn, children are herded into prison-like institutions, forced through threats to unnaturally sit in hard chairs and memorise the most preposterous bits of disconnected information. They are coerced through punishments and rewards to perform on tests, behave according to arbitrary rules, and not communicate with each other. Their teachers are themselves victimised, forced to play a particular character, to behave and react in particular ways, and to present pre-packaged information in which the teacher has no real interest. This truly bizarre situation is not only failing to produce creative individuals, it is sinking into the abyss of its own violence."

From *The Happy Child: changing the heart of education*
by Steven Harrison ISBN 1-59181-000-0,
Sentient Publications 2002

Correspondence

Thanks for your information about *Education Now*. I particularly liked the feature on damage limitation. Since taking early retirement and redundancy I have done some part-time work for Family Learning. I find myself in the rather incongruous situation where the government (through the Basic Skills Agency) is paying me to run courses to tell the parents about the literacy and numeracy strategies - which I do, but perhaps not quite in the way they intended. I try to get the parents to think about what children are being asked to do, how they learn best and yes, damage limitation. Again and again I find I am greeted with a real sense of relief that at last they are being 'given permission' to acknowledge the things they were feeling all along – that the hoops through which their children are being asked to jump are misguided, that it is 'okay' not to force endless homework on them, that learning should be fun, and so on ... It is of some comfort to know that there are like-minded people around, though the number of despairing teachers I meet in the different schools I go into now is quite overwhelming. The most worrying aspect of it all is the seemingly inexorable march of further uniformity.

Linda Brown

This was the first time I had received any literature on what you do and I was so moved by what I read that I burst into tears at the breakfast table. It is great to know that there are other people out there who think the way I do. I am a teacher with 22 years behind me trying to work in an acceptable way. I am currently working in a new school teaching 3-5s. The school offers flexi-schooling and supports home-schoolers ... I have pulled my eldest son out of his secondary school where he was being bullied and talking about suicide.

Alison (full name and address supplied)

Playing the role of the 'good parent'

by Roland Meighan

The general theory that most secondary schools and plenty of primary schools work to is that parents are potential problems. The task for a school is seen as diagnosing which kind of problem. Is this parent an 'interferer'? Or is this one a 'neglecter'? Or is it one that can be neutralised into a 'spectator', admiring or otherwise.

Four features of the 'good parent' expectation have been noted in the research. The school staff can become negative if any of these is neglected.
1. They should be well informed about the school – not easy given the ambiguity of the clues of brochures, meetings, the grapevine of parent conversations, etc.
2. They must show a strong interest in the school's version of education – which may be low on happiness and high on league table results.
3. They need to read accurately the school's idea of the good parent.
4. They must maintain the impression that they accept and support the school's views.

The last two are not easy. Successful parents avoid the label of 'interferers' whilst actually interfering a great deal by buying private tutors, extra book and on-line courses. Schools with high league table rating are usually those with the highest incidence of private tutor purchase. The staff hope it is their activity that makes the difference, but the research suggests otherwise.

(Based on Sharp, R. and Green, A. (1975) *Education and Social Control*, London: Routledge and Kegan Paul)

On the need for parents to become researchers

by Roland Meighan

From *Natural Learning and the Natural Curriculum, part two 'Parents'*

Twenty educationalists including home-based educators, head teachers, industrialists and researchers, met at the University of Nottingham in the Autumn of 1997. They spent two days exchanging ideas on the theme of education in the year 2020. One thing everybody agreed on straightaway was that the climate of uncertainty, due to continuous change, would not go away. **Continuous adaptation was here to stay.**

In this situation, parents who are wanting damage limitation will have to become active members of the learning society themselves, and become constant researchers. By this, I do not mean writing research papers, but asking questions and sifting evidence and any offered answers. Tolstoy suggested that the only real objective of education was *to create the habit of continually asking questions.* (Governments and business are not always disposed to agree, finding passive, gullible minds more acceptable.)

There is another reason why parents need to become researchers. A few years ago, a student on a Master's Degree in Education course became wearied by the constant procession of research studies presented week after week. He asked me to tell him what, in my opinion, all the studies told us in the end. I asked for time to think about it. Next week I gave a verdict. *"What they tell us,"* I declared, *"is that we do not know how to do it. We do not know how to educate children in a complex and changing world. If we knew, we would not have to research it any more. All the research is doing is trying to find useful clues."*

This statement still holds good. But we do have more and better clues than before, especially from the home-based educators. But it means that parents do not have to believe over-confident teachers and educationalists, just as patients do not have to believe over-confident nurses and doctors. We need to sift the evidence for ourselves.

But, asking questions may lead to unexpected conclusions and actions. Those reluctant educational heretics, the home-based educators, decided that they could make decisions based on their own experience and the available evidence, even if they were at odds with 'professional' opinion. They may have even come to the same conclusion as George Bernard Shaw who proposed that *"all professions are conspiracies against the laity"*; well, some of the time anyway, if not most of the time in some cases.

One danger of parents thinking for themselves is that they may be regarded as eccentric. We can take comfort from the words of Bertrand Russell when he said that we should not fear to be eccentric in thought, because *every idea that is now taken for granted, was once said to be eccentric.* It is not the case, however, that being unorthodox guarantees that you are right. There are many possibilities for error, and plenty of unorthodox ideas are dubious, or prove to be just plain wrong.

Becoming a researcher is a permanent state, because in the situation of continuous change, solutions are likely to be temporary expedients. The task might often be to decide the lesser of evils rather than achieve any certain answer. Or the task may be to replace familiar skills with new ones. The computer field illustrates this well. When I wrote a book with my Amstrad 8256, I thought learning all the new skills was well worthwhile. Before long I needed to learn again to work with a PC and Word for Windows. Now I have learnt the new skills needed for my voice-driven computer.

One shortcut for parents to become well-briefed in educational ideas is to be found in the use of quotations. For example, when Mark Twain said that he *"never allowed schooling to interfere with his education"*, he drew attention to a number of propositions. One is that schooling and education are not the same thing, and can often be entirely opposed. Another is that your own private investigations, conducted in your own time and in your own way, can be valid education. Indeed, one of the reasons why schooling and education can be in opposition is that the questions and concerns of the learner can gradually become replaced by the official questions and concerns imposed by others and, even more oppressive, the officially approved answers.

For a second example, take the quotation from George Bernard Shaw when he says: *"What we want to see is the child in pursuit of knowledge, not knowledge in pursuit of the child."* This quotation alerts us to a fundamental objection to a national curriculum or any adult-imposed curriculum. It turns learning into a 'child-hunt' where knowledge hounds the child rather than a 'knowledge-hunt' where learners are encouraged, supported and advised in their seeking out of knowledge. Because I found quotations to be such a powerful aid to thinking, I compiled a book of quotations on education. People tell me it is useful to stimulate discussion, question assumptions, and expose myths and superstitions.

Another shortcut is the use of analogies. When people say that we should learn and memorise things which may be useful to us in the future, we can try to think of other examples of when things are done now in the hope that they may be useful later. The activity of squirrels comes to mind. They collect nuts, bury them and then try to locate them later. Are we being asked to believe that children should collect adult-designated nuts of information, then bury them in their memory, in the hope that they may need to dig them out later? Is this the most effective way to spend time?

For another analogy, Edward Fiske, former New York Times Education Editor, concluded that getting more learning out of our present schooling system was *"like trying to get the Pony Express to beat the telegraph by breeding faster ponies"*. An analogy like this alerts us to the ancient nature of mass schooling and its growing obsolescence due to slowness to adapt. Perhaps tinkering with the system is like getting the stagecoach to go faster by strapping roller skates on the hooves of the horses, when what is needed is a new kind of transport altogether, such as a railroad.

Although it is helpful to locate useful sources of information, I think it was Winston Churchill who said it is better to read wisely than widely. You could read every newspaper every day, but I doubt if it would be worth the effort, and it is better to choose one that does not insult your intelligence. One useful source of information is *ACE Bulletin* from the Advisory Centre for Education, set up to advise parents, at Unit 1B, Aberdeen Studios, 22 Highbury Grove, London N5 2EA (Tel: 020 7354 8318).

Finally, the title of 'parents as researchers' is, perhaps, misleading. It might well read 'families as researchers' since adults and children alike will need this mentality to cope with our ever-changing world and our own slow-to-adapt schooling system. In addition, **purposive conversation** among family members and others, about these and other matters, is one of the most effective ways of learning known.

Part five:

Grandparents
by Michael Foot

(First published as three occasional pieces in Education Now's *News and Review*)

My grandson James, born on June 8th 2001, lives 150 miles away from me. I therefore see him but occasionally. So, when I do see him, his development is obvious and remarkable. Out of his own endeavours, out of his own wish to explore and make sense of his world and with the support of his loving parents, he has developed to such a degree that the newborn baby of just four months ago seems a character of much more distant recall.

Crucially, for all of his four months James has owned his own learning. Those who love him have respected that ownership, have allowed him to determine what he learns, how he learns and the pace at which he learns it; and he has done his learning on the basis of what is useful to him and fun for him. Everybody else has properly seen their role as being to support that learning. In consequence, the amount of learning that James has accomplished is phenomenal.

My fear is that when he is old enough for school, his ownership of his own learning will be taken from him. Others, who will claim to know best, will decide what he has to learn, how he should learn it and how long he should have to do it – in every year of his schooling. And the great and joyful complexity of James's development will be reduced to tick-lists, test scores, targets and grades – which will demean James and demean his learning.

Tucked away in the speech which Tony Blair made at his party's recent conference, was a single paragraph about education. In it, he lamented the fact that 'a quarter of 11-year-olds fail their basic tests'. Yes, he really did speak of 11-year-olds who 'fail' – and I find myself appalled by the suggestion that James might someday merit the label 'failure'. The poverty of our Prime Minister's thinking about education is further illustrated by the fact that his comment about failure at 11 years of age was directly linked to children's potential regarding art and culture:

> *"How many children never know not just the earning power of a good education but the joy of art and culture and the stretching of imagination and horizons which true education brings? Poor education is a personal tragedy and a national scandal. Yet even now, with all the progress of recent years, a quarter of 11-year-olds fail their basic tests and almost half of 16-year-olds don't get five decent GCSEs."*

As if attainments in SATs and GCSEs was a necessary precondition for an engagement with and an appreciation of art and culture! I am surely justified in fearing that such gross misconceptions about the nature of learning will ill-serve James's best interests, just as they ill-serve those children whose schooling is presently constrained by an over-prescriptive and over-tested national curriculum.

Curiously, I would in fact be more confident of James's needs being well served if they were in the hands of my friend Roger. Curiously, because my friend Roger's only direct connection with schools is as chairman of the governors of a secondary school; most of his energies are directed towards running the family building business.

Roger recently took his four-year-old grandson, Aaron, to a centre where the main attractions were the exotic fish in aquariums on the upper floor. But Aaron became most interested in his first experience of the lift which carried them to the upper floor. And Roger was sensitive enough to allow time for Aaron's newly-found interest to be fully satisfied.

Then, when finally they got to the fish and after they had been given a magnifying glass with which to view them, Aaron became most interested in examining his grandfather's eye through the magnifier. He had seen what happened when Roger held it to his eye to demonstrate how to use it. Again Roger was able to allow time for Aaron's curiosity about his magnified eye to be properly satisfied. After which – the fish!

In the light of which, do we really best serve the interests of young children by sending them to be members of relatively large classes in schools where the needs of the individual are generally subordinated to those of the many, and where the needs of the many are decided upon by distant policymakers whose understandings are dangerously limited? Are not those exactly right who argue that it is our youngest children who most need to be in the smallest classes?

So, for the sake of James and his short-term best interests and his lifelong learning, I am for those who respect his ownership of his own learning, who allow his learning to remain rooted in purpose and pleasure, who allow him the time that he needs for his learning, who support him. In conclusion, and if you have stayed with me in the belief that it might be possible for a besotted grandfather to write something other than a eulogy about his first grandson, I offer you some parts of a poem by Oliver Bernard. They say much of what I hope and fear for James's next few years:

You're off to school then in the morning Joe.
This is to say I hope it's not too stupid.
You undertsand, it's this one mainly fears ...
Never be no one, even when completely
Ignored or misconstrued. Don't let discredit
Come upon our old preschool university
Where steam-engines and peacocks were main subjects ...
Be yourself if you can possibly get away with it.

From Verse &c by Oliver Bernard,
Anvil Press Poetry, London 2001

Michael Foot, October 2001

* * * * *

Last year I contributed to *News and Review* a piece *'On Becoming A Grandfather'*. A few people were kind enough to ask about the possibility of further bulletins from the grandfather front. Since my early retirement from primary headship a little over seven years ago, I have kept a journal as a means of 'fixing', of making sense of, and often of celebrating, experience. What follows is my journal entry of Tuesday 2 July 2002 - following a visit to our home in Norfolk by James William, who was by then aged one year and nearly one month.

James and I were together in the sunken garden for about fifteen minutes. This part of our garden is roughly square in shape, its sides being about twelve feet long. I sat on a wooden bench seat on one side of the square. James sat close to my feet on the stone chippings which are spread across the area. Near to him was one of the nine stepping stones, each of them about one foot square, which are distributed haphazardly on top of the chippings. During our time together, I said very little. James paid scarcely any attention to me.

He spent the time absorbed in four activities, moving in no apparent order from one to any one of the others. The four activities were:

- Picking up handfuls of stone chippings and putting them down in a different position.
- Reaching up with handfuls of stone chippings and putting them on the bench seat next to me, and watching as some remained on the slats of the seat and some fell between the slats.
- Picking up handfuls of stone chippings and 'throwing' them or letting them drop onto the square stepping stone which was closest to him; these chippings made a different sound when they landed compared to those that fell onto the main bed of stone chippings.
- Picking up handfuls of stone chippings and letting them fall from his hand onto the main bed of chippings; usually a few chippings had to be persuaded from his hand because they had become caught between his fingers or because they had become stuck to his moist fingers.

And as I watched him engaged in these activities, I was watching a wonderer, an investigator, a discoverer, a marveller. I was watching a learner, owning his own learning, and having the time to wonder, to investigate, to discover, to marvel, to learn.

Since when I have thought about our fifteen minutes together in the context of the way in which too much schooling is arranged - too often without enough ownership, without enough time to wonder, to investigate, to discover, to marvel, to learn.

And today the whole misguided nature of too much schooling became even more frighteningly clear when I came upon the following which was printed on the box of one of the products of a major supplier of educational materials: 'Transform Your Students

Into Problem Solvers & Scientists!' Try telling that to James William Porter - and his grandfather.

Michael Foot, July 2002

* * * * *

Since my last despatch from the grandfather front, Gemma Megan Grace has arrived, a sister for James William. We are therefore enjoying the further delights of watching another young person begin to make sense of and to wonder at her world.

And 'wonder' is entirely the appropriate word. For James William, aged two, the world is like a 'theme park', except that it is not artificially created so as to stimulate and to entertain, but it is - in all its extraordinary ordinariness - full of excitements and adventures and challenges. How I hope that he retains as much as possible of his present dynamically positive approach to the everyday wonderful!

One particular aspect of his recent development has been his graduation at mealtimes from a high chair to a standard chair, complete with cushion, pulled up to the table. He is mostly able to feed himself and any food that falls on the floor is always the result of an accident, never a deliberate act. Recently, however, circumstances when he and his family were visiting friends caused him to be seated for his meal in a high chair. As a response to which, he reverted to throwing his food on the floor. It was a graphic illustration of the combined effect upon behaviour of environment and expectation.

I find myself wondering and worrying about the number of metaphorical high chairs that James and Gemma will be required to sit in when they go to school. Wondering and worrying about how much their development might be hampered by an inappropriate environment and by inappropriate expectations. Like, for example, Key Stage 1 SATs when they are seven.

I recall that when they were first introduced, it was done in such a way that the DES (as was) was able to argue that they would be administered as part of the 'normal' class time and activity, so that children would not be put under any additional stress. By implication, there was an acknowledgement that to conduct SATs for seven-year-olds in a traditional and formal examination would not be in the best interests of children.

Now, even this pretence to serve the best interests of children, this lip service towards children's needs, has been abandoned. I have been made sick at heart and angry to my essence on hearing a detailed description of what happens in Key Stage 1 Reading SATs.

I have heard something about the prescriptive and formalised way that they have to be administered. Something about the right/wrong answers that are asked of the children, questions that demean, even deny, the great imaginative and creative qualities of stories. And then to set all that I have heard within the context of seven-year-olds is to realise the extent of the corruption that has taken place.

Please will politicians and other policy-makers pause a while and think again before they continue to trumpet the 'success' of highest ever reading scores in primary schools. Please will politicians and other policy-makers consider what we lose, what children lose, in a testing and teaching regime which is rooted in 'conform and obey, don't think', where the paths to being 'right' and therefore successful are narrowly confined.

Talking of politicians, did you see the following sentence which appeared in the *Guardian* on Monday 7th July 2003? *"Education will only succeed if pupils are avid learners."* It is such a powerful and important truth that it bears repetition so that it can be savoured more fully:-

> *"Education will only succeed if pupils are avid learners"*.

The words belong to Peter Mandelson. Yes, they belong to Peter Mandelson. And sadly, because of their attribution, I do find in this instance that their great and essential truth is dishonoured, because I am sure that for Mandelson they present little more than grand sounding rhetoric.

I doubt that Mandelson even begins to consider the implications of his great and essential truth. I wonder whether he realises that at birth all children - not just James and Gemma whom I can present as examples – are avid learners. That all children are born avid learners, and therefore successful learners. Does he ever wonder why it is that so many children when they become 'pupils' lose so much of their avidity and become less successful learners? I wonder if Mandelson would understand about metaphorical high chairs!

Thus it is that the mood on this grandfather front remains a mixture of delight and wonder and anxiety. Delight and wonder as I watch the delight and wonder and immense development of early childhood. But delight and wonder combined with an anxiety about the effect that school might have upon that unbounded enthusiasm for life and learning.

Thankfully, this heady cocktail of delight and wonder and anxiety is shared in full measure by James's and Gemma's parents who will, therefore, when necessary, compensate for any worst aspects of their schooling. And dare I hope that there might be the beginnings of a more widespread realisation of the sad and unacceptable realities of our present system, that it might, therefore, improve, might become more humane and more appropriate to children's needs? It's not easy to be optimistic, but I do clutch at possibilities.

Like, for example, the recent report from the commission on human rights of the United Nations, which argues that our current system of testing children at seven, eleven, fourteen and sixteen was designed to fulfil government objectives rather than to meet the needs of children. In an interview, the report's author is quoted as follows:

"Education has to be in the best interests of the child, but it (government policy) is not. It's not about learning, about enabling children to learn and develop, it is about skills in test-taking...

"Whenever testing is introduced it tends to overwhelm the whole design of education. Teachers have to teach the test because that's how children are evaluated and teachers are evaluated. The voice of children is missing."

So there is some reason for hope. And here's some more. The notice which welcomes us to the *Eden Project* in Cornwall describes it as a place which is:

"...all about education but doesn't feel like school."

Says it all, really!

Michael Foot, July 2003

Part six:

Teachers trying to make their classrooms more learner-friendly places

Introduction

by Roland Meighan

John Holt in *Instead of Education* wrote to one young teacher who was asking how he could change the schools:

> *"You are going to have your hands full, just trying to find or make for yourself a spot in which you can do not too much harm, be reasonably honest with your students, help some of them cope a little better with the problems of school, and get some fun out of your work. To do even that little will not be easy."* (p. 209)

Teachers who see themselves as radical rarely changed anything, Holt concluded, and they become frustrated by their failures to teach children to think. They are fooling themselves because they are coerced themselves into doing the business of the school.

It is not likely that a winner-loser society will be radically changed by the winners and as long as school remains compulsory, coercive and competitive, any changes teachers make will be short-lived, or not go very deep, or not spread very far.

Holt suggests that when more of us ask questions about why all adults should be taxed to provide a system of schools from which the children of the rich and affluent gain the most, and what **kind** of schools are we running where the poor children always seem to lose, reform may become possible. In the meantime, teachers can encourage children to have an active learning life outside school:

> *"All the children I have known who were coping best with school, doing well at it, and more or less happy in it, led the largest and most interesting and important parts of their lives outside of school. Children who do not like school and are not*

doing well there, but cannot escape it, need such an out-of-school life even more. And children who escape school must have some alternative, some interesting and pleasant (to them) way of spending the time that other children spend in school."
(p. 215)

In addition the hidden curriculum of the school is best exposed by being honest with children about these matters and expressing healthier values in their own life and work. Often the best thing is to do nothing dramatic, but listen to their children sympathetically, because what a child may need most is what school generally denies them - a chance to tell their story to people who will listen and try to understand. This action by learner-friendly teachers shows that they take their feelings seriously, and this alone may be enough to help their children make the best of it.

Apart from that, teachers can help by showing their children some of the tricks that will help them play the school game better. The children can be helped to realise that the school game is as unreal and abstract as chess, but beating it requires the learning of the tricks. As one said to me, *"Now I know other people think it is senseless too, I can bear it"*. Useless though most of it is, there are rewards of a kind for playing it well, those of college and university entrance and the job tickets.

Participation and democracy in school: and how I found that it always works

by Derry Hannam

For 21 years, as a teacher at all levels of responsibility in state secondary schools, I involved students in as many decision-making processes as I could think of and get away with. I did this because I thought students had a right to have a say and because I thought they would learn more if they did. In fact, I thought they could **only** learn about some things such as justice and democracy in this way.

I watched my first integrated humanities class in a secondary modern school begin to recover from the wicked trauma of 11 plus 'failure' as they struggled to believe that their ideas and interests really mattered to their teacher. The head came into our room one day having heard about the class meetings and the class court. The students were working in shared interest groups on history projects of their own choosing for presentation to the whole class in any media that they thought appropriate. It must have looked pretty wild. He decided to test all ten first-year classes for motivation, general knowledge, and thinking skills with an instrument that I think was called the Bristol Achievement Test. My class scored way ahead of all the others. The head told me *"I instinctively liked what you were doing but I wanted to reassure myself that the kids were learning something as well as having fun"*. **The methods always worked.** Whether I was head of department, head of house, GCSE or A level teacher, participation, choice and responsibility led to ownership, led to self-esteem, led to learning, led to intrinsic and external recognition, led to motivation to participate.

After early retirement I found myself running international seminars on these ideas for the Council of Europe. This led to me being a co-speaker with Bernard Crick at the 1998 Gordon Cook conference in Glasgow. In my talk I argued that citizenship education for democracy must be, at least in part, experiential if there was to be any hope of success. Crick asked me if I could suggest some examples of good practice in state schools. It was a treat to be able to give some recognition to some of the splendid examples that I had collected, which ended up as the 'pink boxes' in the report.

Later we were both speakers with David Blunkett at a conference in Sheffield. I had just come from visiting a school where the head had been giving very public extra resources to the borderline Grade D/C GCSE students to lift the league table position of the school. This had been so blatant that other students who would not get these grades however hard they tried had told me *"this school doesn't want us"*. One girl had said *"I feel that I'm letting the school down because I can't get the grades they need"*. **THEY NEED!** The minister expounded his belief in 'inclusion' apparently unaware of this pernicious effect of league tables. I argued that schools that seriously tried to involve all students in participative activities, seemed to have better than average attendance, fewer exclusions, and better than average GCSE results at 5 A*-G Grades - though not necessarily 5 A*-C. To my surprise, I was asked to carry out a pilot study. I found 12 'more than usually participative' secondary schools in all kinds of catchment areas. They did indeed have fewer exclusions and better 5 A*-G results than the average for 'similar schools' - they also had better results at 5 A*-C. Now I am no great devotee of the merits of the GCSE examination - in fact I am sure much of the content of some courses had little interest or value to some of those students. But something was being learned that was better than *"this school doesn't want me"*. And actually visiting the schools and talking with the students, the self-esteem and ability to communicate with confidence shone through.

Something strange has happened recently. In many ways teaching has become more prescribed, testing has reached insane proportions, exams have become the purpose of education. And yet - **participation is now 'in'. 'Citizenship' has suddenly emerged.**

(The report to the minister can be found at www.csv.org.uk/csv/hannamreport.pdf)

Creating a more learner-friendly (or less learner-hostile) classroom regime

by Philip Toogood

When I began the first of two maternity-leave cover full-time jobs in two different comprehensive schools, in October 2001, I had not taught in a state comprehensive since resigning from my second comprehensive headship in April 1983. I had spent the eighteen years after this in technical 'retirement'. Actually, I was teaching in various alternative education settings. When I retired in 1983 I did so because I thoroughly disagreed with the Thatcher proposals for secondary education and refused to have any part in the development of such a system. I could see this would lead to young people having an experience which would by and large reduce them to the role of those unfortunate French geese that are kept in captivity and fed a diet which qualifies them to be turned into *pâté de foie gras*.

During those eighteen years I had been free to teach with regard to the emerging needs of my students, with respect for their burgeoning intelligences and personal differences, and according to a particular notion of my professional identity as a teacher. It was my job, I thought, to encourage and facilitate their learning so that it would be a transformative, challenging and creative experience. By and large the young people I taught understood our relationship in this sense and did not abuse or take advantage of their freedom to learn. The vast majority seemed to do well in their exams as a by-product of their hard work.

I returned to teaching in the comprehensive system in order to earn money to compensate for personal expenses I had made during the process of closing Flexi-College in July 2000. I also wanted to acquire a small nest-egg from which to hatch other projects in my retirement. Money was my motive and it remained so. In neither school, however, was I able to recapture that essence of learning which I had experienced in the previous eighteen years in alternative settings. I began to wonder why it was that we were so unable to assume that role as a teacher which I had been able to do for the previous eighteen years in alternative education – particularly since in both schools I concluded that students, teachers and parents were evidently yearning for a system which could be more learner-friendly. As people, the teachers, students and parents of each school seemed to me to be wanting something which would really make for a positive and creative experience, but we all seemed incapable of doing much more than to sugar the pill as we went about stuffing the curriculum down their throats in short time-slots between compulsory 'homework'.

On reflection, I conclude that we were unable to make our classrooms more learner-friendly because we and our students were part of a top-down system where others were in authority over us. We were employed to carry out their instructions. Each morning the staff sat in the staff-room at 8.25, to receive our daily briefing from the Head, Deputies and others in 'line management' over us. One memorable morning (in my first school) the Head came in and said, *"I want to cascade down to you my targets for the next few years. I went to my 'appraisal' meeting yesterday and I was told I had to achieve 42% A-Cs at GCSE in two years' time"*. I was appalled by

- the use of the word 'I' (I recalled how in 1660 Louis XIV on his 21st birthday had called his advisers together and said, *"henceforth, messieurs, it is 'moi' who will make the decisions"*)
- the use of the words 'cascade down'
- the notion that *"'I' had to achieve 42%"*.

Who does he think actually does the work? (I said to myself) as I crept out of the staff-room in my charity shop dark suit to go to the staff toilet.

In both schools, I was told by my heads of department that I was to do things a certain way and should not innovate. I was, after all, only there while the regular teacher had a baby. If I succeeded in introducing a more learner-friendly regime this would cause problems when she returned. If I failed it would cause immediate mayhem. So I arrived at 7.30 every morning, prepared my front of class lessons in minute detail and stood with my back to the door on Friday afternoons to prevent them getting out early in case one of them should have a road accident and the responsibility for their being 'loose' before time was traced back to me!

If I took a regular job now, however, I would try to do things differently within the 'system'. For five hours a day, young people are routed round teachers' specialist rooms arriving as late as they dare and leaving as soon as they can. I would try to engineer a situation where the variables of any learning situation are within the control of the students and myself.

These are to do with the organisation of time, territory, things, teamwork and thinking (planning and reviewing). The trouble is that schools are managed today so that all these tools are used *for* students rather than with them or by them.

This is what makes school so learner-hostile. The lesson times are prescribed and the short time during which they flash before an individual teacher in a group of 30 is devoted to 'delivery' by the teacher, usually from the front of the class. The classroom is laid out in an inflexible way, either in rows or a hollow square, so that it is suitable neither for lecturing, whole group discussion, small group interaction, or individual study. Computers usually have their own classrooms in banks of 30 or so and students are routed round these for an hour a week. The resources are carefully hoarded by the teacher in multiple sets which have to be given in at the end of the lesson. Students are usually told which books to use and what pages to refer to.

Usually a teacher teaches alone – maybe with a classroom assistant to sit by a person with special learning difficulties. There is little teamwork – how can there be when the whole organisation is prescribed so that one teacher faces one class for one hour? Planning is done by the teacher before the lesson and work is marked outside class time and given back in class in an atmosphere of simplistic congratulation, condemnation or suspension of judgement by the teacher. Whole class feedback is the norm and personalised reviewing of work is rare.

In spite of this, the fact remains that once the classroom door is shut and the thirty students are in, then the management of learning could be shared by the teacher with the students. This is only possible if the teacher has a professional relationship with the students which identifies the students as being the ones who are learning and doing the work and the teachers as being in support of this self-motivated process.

Making schools more learner-friendly

by Charlie Cooper

Evidence suggests that school for many pupils is an unhappy and meaningless experience (Hendry, in Figes 2002). Sociological explanations of why this is the case point to education's role in maintaining dominant power relationships in capitalist societies (Corrigan 1979; Foucault 1977), requiring it to suffocate prospects for more liberating, innovative, dialogical pedagogical processes, tolerant of difference and diversity (Cooper 2002). As a consequence, schools have an unhealthy tendency to focus on managerialist outcomes – delivering the national curriculum, improving attainment levels and rising up the league table – at the expense of any individual pupil's needs. Drawing on lessons from youth work practice in Britain, this short piece suggests the basis for a more learner-friendly school environment.

School lessons from Youth Work

There is much that schools could learn from traditional youth work practice. For example, one study asking young people what they wanted from their youth service highlighted four perceived needs – association (somewhere they wanted to go); activities (things which were interesting to do); autonomy (a place of their own); and advice (someone trusting who they could talk to) (Williamson et al. 1995). Young people value a place where they feel accepted, respected and listened to - a warm, safe environment within which to interact with peers and achieve a personal sense of identity and self-esteem (Robertson 2002). Schools, therefore, firstly need to reflect on how their own physical and cultural environments mirror these virtues.

Secondly, attention also needs to be given to the teacher-pupil interaction:

> *"Most of the adults that young people meet in their daily lives are authority figures, or are seen as such: teachers, parents, shopkeepers. Young people often expect adults to treat them in certain ways – i.e. as children – and are amazed to be treated as an adult and taken seriously".* (Robertson 2002: 4)

Young people often have positive feelings about youth workers, largely because they feel treated by them as adults (Robertson 2002). Central to this is the opportunity for young people to genuinely participate in decision making. This in itself is not simply an important learning experience - requiring empathy with others, mutual respect, an ability to analyse and reflect, negotiating skills, and so forth – but places democracy at the core of the education process. Education should not simply be about developing intellect and life skills, but the values and virtues needed to engage critically in social and political activities. This requires schools to be open, and to hold less preconceived notions about outcomes and give greater attention to process. It also requires schools to organise their curriculum and the way this is delivered around the interests and enthusiasms of the pupils, identified through dialogue and consensus. The role of the teacher here is 'facilitator of learning' - a trusted adviser able to offer guidance based on her or his experience and theoretical understanding.

Such an approach offers prospects for a more meaningful curriculum, delivered in imaginative ways deploying a range of techniques - exploiting the arts, leisure, community activities and so forth - in different locations; to learn, as Smith names it, 'in community' (Smith 2000: 4). Education becomes a 'process of fostering learning in life as it is lived' (Jeffs and Smith 1999: 7). This also requires accepting the unpredictability of learning – allowing things to be said and developed spontaneously, not in accord with some pre-designed lesson plan.

Finally, schools need more meaningful approaches to evaluating education. The managerialist performance criteria imposed on schools by OFSTED focus on measurable (and dubious) outcomes of success. These serve to impose conformity on schools in order to permit comparisons (in the name of quality enhancement) and open competition. In reality, some educators are fabricating school attainment figures (Smith 2000), making a mockery of claims to quality assurance and standards. Evaluation needs to be more dialogical – negotiated between the key stakeholders (teachers, parents/carers, pupils and so forth). It needs to focus on the quality of the learning experience and how this enhances well-being – qualitative indicators of success rather than merely measuring the measurable. Here schools can learn from youth work practice's emphasis on 'informal education' (Jeffs and Smith 1999), with a greater focus on evaluating the quality of teacher-pupil interactions. This might include asking such questions as:

- how were learners most effectively stimulated?
- were agreed aims achieved?
- were agreed outcomes achieved?
- what effect has the learning process had on the pupils' collective sense of well-being?

Conclusions

Since the post-war years, discourses of 'youth' - from the 'unruly teenagers' of the Beatnik era to the 'feral youth' of today - have problematised the behaviour and activities of young people. Whilst such constructions of the young can be explained as 'moral panics' (Cohen 1980) - the amplification of deviance to legitimate further coercive measures of state social control - should we not reverse this discourse and question the ability of our social system - including education - to equip our young adequately for adulthood? Much of the evidence suggests that the school system is failing to meet the social, emotional and psychological needs of our children (Figes 2002). Indeed, the crude and narrow performance regime imposed on schools is having brutal effects in terms of increased anxiety levels among children and undermined teacher morale (Smith 2000). At the same time, it is encouraging the massaging of school performance levels. The system is clearly in crisis, corrupt and humanly damaging, and we are all victims of its tyrannical practices. Education needs to be reclaimed as a liberalising, democratising and humanising force, one that fosters genuine notions of inclusion, tolerance and justice. To say that this cannot be done because central state control and surveillance precludes action, is not an acceptable excuse. The recommendations set out above are not particularly radical and certainly achievable. Moreover, as E.P. Thompson observed in *The Making of the English Working Class*, individuals and groups are conscious human agents. We have the ability to resist the oppressive practices of our existing education system. Apart from the damage it is doing to educators themselves, the abuse it is imposing on our children alone should provide the incentive. It is time to think the unthinkable!

References

Cohen, S. (1980) *Folk Devils and Moral Panics: the Creation of Mods and Rockers,* 2nd. Edn, New York: St. Martin's Press.

Cooper, C. (2002) *Understanding School Exclusion: Challenging Processes of Docility,* Nottingham: Education Now/University of Hull.

Corrigan, P. (1979) *Schooling the Smash Street Kids,* London and Basingstoke: Macmillan.

Figes, K. (2002) *The terrible teens: what every parent needs to know,* London: Penguin Viking.

Foucault, M. (1977) *Discipline and Punish: The Birth of the Prison,* Harmondsworth: Penguin.

Jeffs, T. and Smith, M.K. (1999) *Informal Education - conversation, democracy and learning,* 2nd Edn., Ticknall: Education Now.

Robertson, S. (2002) 'A warm, safe place: an argument for youth clubs', *Youth & Policy,* 70, www.infed.org/archives/e-texts/robertson_clubs.htm.

Smith, M.K. (2000) *Youth Work Beyond Connexions,* www.infed.org/personaladvisers/beyond-connexions.htm.

Williamson, H., Afzal, S., Eason, C. and Williams, N. (1995) *The needs of young people aged 15-19 and the Youth Work Response,* Caerphilly: Welsh Youth Agency.

Lost in space: disorientated children, damaged learners

by Ben Koralek

An indoor working environment which can be ice-cold *and* like a tropical Palm-house on the same day is all too familiar for children and teachers working in school buildings across the UK.

The huge, three-storey Victorian, gable-ended castle of a building in which I used to work is plagued too by many of the typical problems of poor acoustics, glare (from un-shaded, double-height windows) and cramped circulation conditions for its 450-strong child population.

The same building's windows are stuck shut by layers of paint work, which - over the years - have sealed those elements of the school's architecture designed specifically to help regulate air quality, to provide smoke ventilation in case of fire and to prevent a build-up of warm, moist, stagnant air (ideal for infectious bacteria seeking to multiply).

Whilst for some, this image of a sickly, antiquated monolith creaking with design and technical problems might serve as an analogy for the whole contemporary schooling 'machine', others would settle for a more straightforward diagnosis of Sick Building Syndrome.

Either way, we cannot escape the simple truth that the nature and condition of a school's built environment can damage both a child's physical health *and* their experience of learning. As Tim Brighouse points out (writing in the TES in 2002): 'the annual report of Her Majesty's Chief Inspector always recorded evidence that one in five poor lessons could be attributed to the state of school buildings.'

As well as hindering children's learning and - perhaps more tellingly - adults' teaching, *"the buildings available for schooling [also] imply psychological, philosophical, sociological and pedagogical ideas about schooling that are often taken for granted"*. (Meighan, R. & Siraj-Blatchford, I. (2003) *A Sociology of Educating,* London: Continuum)

We certainly still take for granted the idea that a classroom is the best space for teaching and learning. That the building's accommodation and classroom layout determine what learning activities are feasible with a class of thirty pupils means that children's learning is limited just as much by the confined space (that typifies so many classrooms in both Primary and Secondary school buildings), as it is by the logistics of working with up to 35 young people simultaneuosly.

Despite the success and insight of recent Multiple Intelligence (MI) research (www.pz.harvard.edu/sumit), far too few classroom learning opportunities are made available for those young people who are readily identifiable as predominantly suited to **bodily-**

kinesthetic, spatial, naturalist or **musical core operations** modes of learning (for example).

Even those class teachers prepared to adapt their current practice in accordance with Howard Gardner's MI theory find it difficult to modify their own classroom space in any meaningful way (Gardner, 1983). Whilst a former colleague of mine has created a small, corner-space in her classroom for a few 'bodily-kinesthetic' learners, it is not straightforward for teaching staff to deliver bespoke learning programmes in a range of organised spaces, for thirty individual pupils, in one room, at the same time! Even the latest classroom designs struggle to accommodate such a range of learning styles (DfES (2002) *Schools For The Future*, Building Bulletin 95).

Coupled with this are the behavioural expectations which many teachers feel obliged to enforce in order to best deliver aspects of the National Curriculum. The (perhaps unreasonable) expectation on Primary children's ability to sit calmly and patiently on a carpet during 'Literacy Hour' for up to twenty minutes at a time is a good example of this.

On the one hand we fail to provide appropriate spatial arrangements for children with a diverse range of educational needs and, on the other - whilst presenting them with a ready-made homogenised curriculum - we make unreasonable demands on their attention, energy and physical stamina.

This combination of conditions damages children's self-esteem and, for some, distorts their highly personal experience of learning to the extent that they become educationally 'disorientated'.
Alongside this, whether sitting still or moving around the school building (or embarking on the repeated transitional 'journeys' from highly-regulated indoor spaces to much less-regulated external spaces and back again, for example), children's relationships with their school building can also be highly disorientating.

Whilst some children manage to steer their way through these complexities, others, become, 'lost' in space; disconnected and isolated from the social and learning environment around them. Children already displaced and disorientated in emotional and/or cultural terms can be especially sensitive to their physical environment. For them, *"to be disorientated in space is to be psychotic"*. (Hall, E. (2000) *The New Learning Environments*, Dudek Architectural Press.)

If we are to minimise this kind of damaging experience for children and young people, we must give more time and consideration to the way we design, organise and animate learning environments within existing school buildings.

Whilst we are yet to see a mainstream UK school commit itself to incorporating MI theory in the organisation of their learning environment/s and curriculum planning, one Scottish school has found a way to create a whole new kind of learning environment: a learning studio which pupils in years 6 and 7 are free to visit whenever they want (if their classwork is up to date).

As well as being a flexible working space in which **spatial, bodily-kinesthetic, intrapersonal** and **interpersonal** learners can flourish, 'Room 13' at Caol Primary School in Fort William is *"run by the children as an autonomous republic, independent of the school. It elects its own officials, keeps its own accounts and pays [artist-in-residence] Rob Fairley his salary"*; making it, in MI theory terms, an ideal context for **linguistic** and **logical-mathematical** learners (John Crace, The Guardian, 18/6/2002).

Sadly, imaginative educational and spatial innovations of this kind, are few and far between. Not every school has an additional or spare room that it is able to dedicate to a wide range of creative activities for small group work, on a fixed basis. Instead, many schools perceive themselves as cramped in their buildings: stuck for extra space, and therefore unable to organise their working environment to better suit the educational needs of their pupils. As a result, as many teachers will acknowledge, architectural and spatial limitations crystallize behaviour problems for a significant number of children.

Indeed, schools which dedicate specific support and in-school interventions (either from Learning Support Assistants, Occupational Therapists, Speech & Language Therapists, Child Psychologists and Learning Mentors, for example) do so - to a certain extent - in order to compensate for the lack of creative thought which might otherwise go into re-designing a more effective and child-responsive learning environment.

If we are to limit the damage inflicted on our children from overexposure to poorly 'tuned' learning environments, we might start by asking ourselves (as members of one London local authority's Primary Learning Support Service do of school staff):

> *"Have you offered a change of location or setting, e.g. a smaller space, a low distraction area, and have you adapted the environment to support the individual?"*

We can't escape surveillance, but we can, at least, evade the thought police

by Clive Erricker

Language is like fire. Both are regarded as human inventions or as natural phenomena to be put to human purpose. Both are violent, in the sense used by Bourdieu, in that they produce change. Concepts are like atoms - they are the basis of the activity of fire and the activity of communication. With fire we can create warmth and we can create bombs. It is powerful and dangerous and alive. Concepts can be weapons and they can be empowering notions: powerful, dangerous and alive. Within communication they can be used against us, to limit us or to liberate us.

Every document I read that comes from a centralised agency and regulating authority contains the same core concepts: training, standards, levels, attainment, development and failure. This, as Foucault observed, is the mechanism of surveillance. How to be under surveillance and yet think and act as though you were free, that is the question.

So far I have presented a picture of schooling based on a particular metaphor: surveillance. Concepts are always metaphorical in nature but they shape the social 'reality'. This concept is anti-educational if we regard education as something that should be liberating. But what if I translate these concepts into a different educational metaphor of 'liberation', which I want to spiritually and mentally inhabit? I am suggesting we can do this provided our energies are not already sufficiently drained. I can only make sense of and be energised by the idea of teaching if I do this.

When I read a piece of 'surveillance speak' (and here it relates to my specialist subject, religious education): *"Assessment of pupils' performance which is comparatively weak in most subjects, is a particular weakness in RE"*, I experience the concept of 'assessment' being aimed at me and the trigger is fired. We already anticipate the next inspection and the feelings engendered are depression and anxiety. Here I am not condoning a lack of assessment but, when delivered in this way, assessment is a brutal word: hard and unforgiving; cutting through the difference between the divisive poles of success and failure, but, let me translate. What do I want to do with young people? I want to engage them, challenge and support them, help them to own a sense of their own education and experience the satisfaction and empowerment in being able to express their understanding in their own way. I want them to gain their own voice. I cannot do this unless I ask them to express themselves, analyse, discuss and reflect. That is what I see as the job of a teacher. 'Assessing' is what both they, the pupils, and I do in this process. If, at the fag end of it, I have to tie up a bundle for Ofsted to consume, using their terms but given my meaning, so be it. I have my own ownership of 'assessment' within my metaphor of education as liberation, and I want young people to develop theirs - because I do not want them to be objects of assessment.

Here is an example of assessment we can make, in the classroom, on those who would like to control our thinking for their benefit. It is, perhaps, instructive that Ofsted themselves are now sending out a message that over-assessment is bad practice, and that 'assessment for learning' is the appropriate term which involves pupils' assessment of their own performance. (Is this an admission that the initial instruction backfired due to it being an instruction?)

Right now, I walk into my newsagent and see a poster for the National Lottery. It contains a slogan: 'everybody wins' with a picture of a smiling child and a logo of two hands shaking each other. This strikes me as a valuable 'resource'. Who wins? First, very few people, compared to those who pay for a ticket, get a return. Second, how many 'charities' actually get a grant compared to those who apply or need the money? Same answer. Third, who gets a huge and continuing profit? The people in charge of the national lottery: the corporation. Sounds to me like free-market capitalist competition. Maybe the slogan should say 'We must all compete'.

I can have great fun with a class 'assessing' this poster and I can put their 'performance' in the box under a number of headings: from literacy skills to citizenship education, from values education to thinking skills. We can debate each other's interpretations and we can challenge each other's conclusions. Most importantly, our classroom becomes a site to initiate change (as Bordieu observed). You see, **maybe we can't escape surveillance, but we can, at least, evade the thought police.**

* * * * *

Note: Clive Erricker is expressing his own views not those of Hampshire County Council.

Part seven:

Damage Limitation: the Do-it-yourself Approach

by Hazel Clawley

"I have never allowed schooling to interfere with my education," said Mark Twain. He is not alone in this. Probably every contributor to this volume could make a similar claim – though some of us might need to change the 'never' to 'seldom'. The miracle is that so many people do, in fact, survive the school system with the *"holy curiosity of inquiry"* (Einstein) still alive, with a reasonable ability to relate to and work with others, and with no illusions about the dubious value of the years of compulsory schooling they have endured.

This must be because they have practised their own form of damage limitation. It may be that they have been helped by sympathetic parents, teachers or other adults, as described elsewhere in this book. But my contention is that, with or without such help, children and young people often develop their own methods of damage limitation, which we should recognise and celebrate.

This is not to deny the terrible damage that schooling can inflict on many children. I know this from personal experience. We withdrew our own son from school at the age of seven, after three increasingly painful years. Some of the scars are still there: our only regret is that we sent him to school at all. He might not have been a survivor.

But I survived, and so did those who are now most critical of the compulsory schooling system. What did we do? And what do children do now? In what follows I draw on many years of working with people who found school difficult, and listening to their experiences. I have worked with children attending after-school clubs; also through *Education Otherwise*, with children who were eventually withdrawn from school; and, as an adult education tutor, with adults who found school particularly trying because their dyslexia was not recognised.

First, look at school itself. In class, if the topic or the style of teaching have no value for pupils, they opt out mentally. Increasingly draconian punishments await their parents if they are not physically present in their seats but (as yet) there is no thought police. They use the time for their own daydreaming, thinking, planning, resting. They observe the dynamics of the class, watch what the others are doing, assess whether anyone else is gaining any benefit from the event, and if so, why – all the while, apparently, paying attention to the official business of the lesson and, for most of the time, keeping out of trouble. More boldly, and more riskily, they stare out of the window to aid their daydreaming, they (discreetly) read literature of their own choosing, they jot down their own thoughts on topics remote from the business of the class, but important to them. All of these redeeming strategies, and more besides, are used by many of us when, as adults, we find ourselves inadvertently trapped in a boring training session or meeting. They are grown-up, sensible ways of behaving. Yet most schools and teachers do not recognise this, let alone give credit for it.

Still in class, pupils may pay close attention to the subject-matter of the session, whether or not it has any immediate interest or relevance, purely as an exercise in thinking and questioning. Is what is being said reasonable, logical? What evidence is presented? The questioning can be purely in the mind, jotted down on paper, or, if occasion offers, shared with the class. The last option can be dangerous. Many teachers do not value this Socratic approach to learning, and will dismiss it as insolence – which, in part, it may actually be. Other teachers will value it as the point at which the session comes alive, and real learning begins.

Co-operative strategies are sometimes used as damage limitation. Pupils who are bored because a session moves too slowly for them, or because they have already fully explored the topic on the internet or through their own reading, will help and support their friends who are not coping well with the subject-matter or the set exercises. Even today, this is sometimes frowned on in class, and may have to be done surreptitiously – but it should be recognised as a truly creative way of coping with what could otherwise be many wasted hours. The other side of this coin is the equally sensible and praiseworthy efforts of struggling pupils to elicit help from friends in the class – still sometimes dismissed by teachers, in competition-ridden classrooms, as 'copying' or 'cheating'.

School, like most of our institutions, is governed by rules and punishments, with the occasional reward. Very few schools are in any way democratic. Rules and punishments are usually decided by the head teacher, sometimes with help from other senior teachers and governors. How do children and young people practise damage limitation when confronted with rules which often seem silly and pointless? All this in the context of a system which flies in the face of all they are taught (in the classroom, as well as through the media) about the value of democracy, and its central place in our national life.

The first and most overbearing rule, made and (increasingly) enforced by central government rather than by the school, is that pupils have to be physically present in the school building, unless they have official permission to be elsewhere. This has recently been extended to forbid family holidays during school term-time. Children and young people who find school impossible to cope with, for a variety of very good reasons explored elsewhere in this book, often practise emergency damage limitation simply by breaking the first rule, and not turning up. Some are canny enough to register first, and then escape. Research has shown that many absent themselves only on specific days when some particularly horrendous challenge awaits them in the form of a sarcastic teacher, or a subject in which they are struggling, or the experience of having to undress in front of others in the changing room or showers, or a confrontation with bullies among their peer group.

Where parents understand and empathise with their child's fear and dislike of school, they may be able to work with the school to solve some of these problems, write some timely sick notes as a holding operation, or even investigate the possibility of a change of school, or of home-based education. They must act fast, or new repressive legislation may have them behind bars.

Where parents don't understand, or don't know what to do about the situation, what options do such children have? I suggest that truancy – viewed as the refusal of young people to place themselves day after day in humiliating, frightening or simply pointless situations - is a valid emergency damage limitation exercise. Of course, such children may be at risk from other dangers, especially if they are afraid to go home during school hours. And sooner or later, town or city children are likely to be picked up by one of the new truancy patrols whose function is to chase them back to the oppressive institution from which they have temporarily escaped.

What kind of society are we creating, where for so many children the choices set before them are between various kinds of fear, humiliation or boredom? Truancy – occasional, or regular - may not be the best form of damage limitation, but for some it is the only one on offer.

Those who decide that school attendance is unavoidable, or even worthwhile for some of the time, develop ways of coping with unreasonable rules and forms of discipline. Successful strategies might be summed up as follows:

- keep the rules if you can (and if you know what they are, which is not always clear);
- if you break a rule, try not to get caught;
- if you challenge or question a rule or a disciplinary procedure, try to do so politely and reasonably, and if possible on behalf of someone else, rather than in your own defence;
- get to know your rights under the law and under the UN Convention on the Rights of the Child, and quote them where serious matters are at stake.

Some of the time spent in the school buildings or grounds is 'free' time: lunch time and breaks, intervals between lessons. What makes school bearable for many children, and tips the balance between wanting or not wanting to attend, is the friendship and free play of these all too brief in-between times. These are the elements of the school experience which home-educated children often miss the most when first withdrawn from school. School survivors are often those who know how to make the most of the relationships forged 'in the gaps': the shared interests and hobbies, the conversations (often frowned on in class), the skills developed, the secrets shared. As with damage limitation in the classroom, this is a familiar situation to adults attending training days or conferences. It is perfectly acceptable for adults to state that the most fruitful parts of a conference were the conversations with colleagues over coffee or in the bar. A child making similar claims in a class discussion on 'the value of school' might well be taken to task by the teacher for demonstrating a frivolous approach to education.

School occupies a large part of children's lives. But, as Roland Meighan demonstrated in Part One, once the school day (and the homework) is over, and also at week-ends and in the long holidays, there are many more hours left for living and learning, and for undoing some of the damage caused by the current over-prescribed and narrow school curriculum. He describes activities typical of many families learning together: clubs, outings, projects. But what of those children whose families do not function like this? Can they – do they – find positive ways to learn more about the real world than the limited school curriculum allows? Or is this form of damage limitation for well-adjusted, middle-class families only?

In my experience, some children do seek out and find positive alternatives to school learning, even though much of their out-of-school learning about the world may be very negative indeed. Peer-groups may become gangs, and children rejected by school and neglected by family may find themselves drawn into such close and loyal networks and so into crime and danger. But there are positive choices made, too. Children still join the public library of their own volition. They know how to make the most of the information-rich society in which they live. The TV set continually playing in the corner of the room can still be a window on the world. Computer games develop hand-eye co-ordination, and often other skills besides. The interests and hobbies shared in the school playground spill over into after-school hours. In my inner-city patch, street-play still survives, with creative ball games making the most of the spaces available, skateboarding, cycling and scootering. Older children may brave the park, and use for free the climbing wall (when the custodian is otherwise engaged), watching and learning from the skilled adult climbers. Children and young people are eternally creative in using the fabric of the city to entertain themselves, and learn in the process. The French phenomenon of 'free running' is a recent example of a breathtaking new sport invented by city kids, who leap, run and dance over urban landscapes and buildings.

Children can also seek out more structured settings for enriching their after-school hours. I have helped to run clubs and activities for children and teenagers in several inner-city areas. At one centre, in east London, we conducted a series of interviews in which children spoke freely about their school experiences. Most of those interviewed had little that was good to say about their schools. Some liked the sports – that was all. Many attended school only sporadically.

They had found the centre – in the High Street – without any help from adults. Having found it, and liked what it offered, their attendance was **very** regular, to the extent of trying desperately to talk their way in on nights when the centre was not open for activities. The team of youth workers and volunteers wanted to run the club in a democratic way, based around a weekly meeting of all involved. This was hard work. At first the idea was met with incredulity. *"It's your club, innit? You tell us what to do, fix up outings, get us games and stuff, and we join in."* The meetings were voted 'boring' by many, and avoided. But some understood the idea of making decisions about their own club, appreciated this unique taste of democracy in a life where they were 'pushed around' by one adult after another, and started to take it seriously.

Whether or not the lessons in practical democracy made sense, the club's activities certainly enriched the experience of kids most of whom had not travelled far from their own part of east London. They enjoyed the usual children's club activities of arts and crafts, music, drama, cookery, with camping and rock-climbing trips as special events. They appreciated a place to hang out in, especially in the winter – just somewhere warm and dry to sit around and talk, with no pressure. Sometimes, when invited, the adults would join in the conversations. The group who persevered with the weekly meeting voted to do a major re-design and decorating job on the club basement: they made the decisions, within the slender budget available, and did the work, with support from older volunteers. They were learning many practical skills. They were also learning how to make decisions and work co-operatively in an atmosphere of mutual respect.

Adults who respected and listened to children, instead of shouting and pushing them around, were a new and strange phenomenon, not always trusted at first. There must be a catch. The staff must be 'wallies' or 'divs', especially working for the rock-bottom wages paid by the voluntary organisation funding the club, or even working for nothing, in the case of several volunteers. The out-of-school lessons learned in the family and peer-group culture of that part of London – that there is always a catch, that no one helps you without a payback, that you should grab what you can when you can – were hardly a constructive counterbalance to lessons learned in school. The habit of 'nickin' was endemic with some of the children: they stole from their own club, they stole from staff, they stole from shops when taken on outings. What was new was that, on occasion, they shamefacedly admitted what they had done, and gave the items back.

I have worked in several such clubs, centres and playschemes in inner-city areas in London, Leeds and Birmingham. All credit to the children who, in spite of school failure and family indifference, seek out their own means of damage limitation. For those who do not, the downward spiral of failure, rejection and violence – against themselves or against others – will continue. **The answer is ultimately political: we need a learning system which itself seeks to limit the damage inflicted on many children by poverty, a bleak physical environment, parental neglect or family upheavals: a learning system which is flexible and life-enhancing, which values, respects and nurtures children, and which celebrates their individuality, creativity and sheer joie de vivre.**

Part eight:

Schooling can seriously damage your health: education for violence, education for peace

From the inaugural lecture at University of Birmingham, May 2002

by Professor Clive Harber

I want to make a personal statement about education – to draw on personal experience, my own research and my reflection on the work of others to present some ideas about what is wrong and potentially right about education. In particular I want try to get away from the many technical issues that pass as educational debate these days to look at more fundamental questions surrounding the basic purposes of education – what sort of individuals and what sort of societies are we trying to create?

Generally, it is assumed that formal education is necessarily and inherently a 'good thing', that it is a key indicator of development and that what happens inside schools and higher education is automatically of benefit to both individuals and society. This assumption is shared, most of the time, by national governments, global institutions like the World Bank and international aid agencies who expend a great deal of time and effort trying to get more children into school and keep them there with only an occasional hint in their literature that all might not be well within schooling itself. The problem is that this literature is overwhelmingly concerned with rights *to* education rather than rights *in* education. Hence, the enormous global expenditure on formal education and the major conference held at Jomtien, Thailand in 1990, when most governments of the world met to plan how they would provide universal primary education for all children by the year 2000. It was followed by a similar conference held in Dakar, Senegal in

2000 where they met again to explain why they had not achieved their targets for 2000 but promised to do so by 2015.

But is it true? Is formal education necessarily or always good for you or your society? There is little point in providing education for all, meaning most of the time schooling for all, unless it is going to do more good than harm. In the first part of this lecture I want to argue that **education as it has been, and is, organised in the shape of primary and secondary schools, has too often been harmful**. It is my contention that this negative dimension of schooling has been consistently played down or ignored in governmental policy documents and academic writing and research. Yet until we recognise what is wrong, we cannot start to put it right.

My main concern, however, is more clear-cut – how and why have schools actually been harmful to young people and society? In particular, I will be concerned with some of the ways in which schools have been violent to pupils and have helped to perpetuate violence in the wider society. So, while there has been much attention in the media on the violence of pupils towards teachers in schools, this lecture looks at the other side of the coin but will also argue that there is a nevertheless a relationship between the two. I must stress, especially as there are teachers in the audience, including some who are my relatives, that the intention is very definitely **not** to blame any group such as teachers or lecturers, but to explore what it is about schooling *as a system* that can lend itself to a violent and oppressive interpretation. Teachers, lecturers and administrators are often victims of education systems in the same way that pupils are.

There was a television programme broadcast in January 2002 which was called *Conspiracy*. The TV guide to the programme started the description of the programme in the following way:

> *"A dramatisation of the meeting that took place in Berlin on January 20th 1942 in which a roomful of well-educated lawyers sat down to a lavish dinner, with brandy and cigars, and voted to gas the entire Jewish population of the western hemisphere."*

Hence for me the importance of the following letter which was sent by a USA High School Principal to his teachers at the beginning of every academic year. It concerns education under the Nazis in Germany. Some of you may have heard this before, and indeed I have been using it since 1984, but it is one of the most powerful reminders of the evil that the wrong sort of education can do, so I make no apologies for using it one more time – especially in the light of the increasing success of the far right across Europe at the moment.

> *"Dear Teacher, I am the survivor of a concentration camp. My eyes saw what no man should witness. Gas chambers built by learned engineers, children poisoned by educated physicians, infants killed by trained nurses, women and babies shot and burned by high school graduates. So I am suspicious of education. My request is, help your children become more human. Your efforts must never produce learned monsters, skilled psychopaths, educated Eichmans.* **Reading, writing and arithmetic are important only if they serve to make our children more human.**"

From more recent times there is the religious violence that has taken place in India. In March 2002 a crowd of 10,000 Hindus dragged a Muslim M.P., his brother-in-law, his brother-in-law's wife and their two small sons into the street from their house and set them alight. The Police Commissioner for the city where it happened stated, *"I hang my head in shame. The people responsible for all this come from the better sections of society. They are not criminals. Many of them are educated..."*. In South Africa, right up to the end of the 1980s, highly 'educated', or perhaps more accurately qualified, medical doctors were involved in cases of torture of political prisoners under the apartheid regime. Of the five men identified in a newspaper article as being closest to the French neo-fascist Presidential contender Jean-Marie Le Pen, two are law professors at French universities and two were described as having 'brilliant' minds – and this was in the Guardian newspaper! In the Rwandan genocide of 1994 when between 800,000 and a million people (one eighth of its population) were murdered in the space of a few weeks, teachers from a Hutu ethnic background commonly denounced their Tutsi pupils to the militia or even directly killed them themselves. Indeed, the role of schooling in this genocide poses some very serious and important questions about why and how we educate in all societies. As two commentators on the Rwandan genocide put it,

"The role of well-educated persons in the conception, planning and execution of the genocide requires explanation; any attempt at explanation must consider how it was possible that their education did not render genocide unthinkable. The active involvement of children and young people in carrying out the violence, sometimes against their teachers and fellow pupils, raises further questions about the kind of education they received".

I hope, through these examples, that I have made the point **that schooling is not automatically a good thing and that everything depends on its political and moral purposes and its resulting practices**. In this regard it is important to note that in the history of state provided mass education there has always been a tension between education for political control on the one hand and education for liberation and critical awareness on the other. It is my view that, unfortunately, the control function has almost always significantly had the upper hand. It is certainly the case that one of the main purposes for the introduction of modern mass schooling in Europe at the end of the nineteenth century, was social and political control, particularly of a potentially troublesome organised working population – what we used to call the working class. As Marten Shipman put it in his study of education and modernisation,

"Punctuality, quiet orderly work in groups, response to orders, bells and timetables, respect for authority, even tolerance of monotony, boredom, punishment, lack of reward and regular attendance at place of work are the habits to be learned at school."

Thus authoritarian control and surveillance have always been a significant part of modern mass schooling and this model was extended globally from European societies through colonisation where the purpose of schooling was to help control indigenous populations for the benefit of the colonial power. By the 1930s colonialism had exercised its sway over 85 % of the world.

In terms of control and surveillance the first thing to note about much of schooling is the element of **compulsion**. Yet many children for much of the time do not want to be in school in the first place. The essentially coercive nature of this forced approach to education was recently stressed by John Cosgrove, a deputy headteacher with over twenty years' experience in primary and secondary schools, who wrote:

> *"Let's not kid ourselves. Even in the easiest, best motivated schools, many of the pupils, much of the time, would rather not be there. Children do not choose to go to school. The choice is made for them. Once in school, more or less unwillingly, pupils are presented with activities chosen for them and they are given no option about attempting them. There do exist schools where pupils have a free choice about which lessons to attend, and whether or not they complete assignments, but such institutions are as rare as primroses flowering on an English New Year's Day. For the most part schools make children do things."*
> (Cosgrove, 2001: 51).

Indeed, the extent to which schools and other agencies will go to get pupils into school is really quite extraordinary and involves some stick and some carrot. On the carrot side, one school in Halifax, U.K., is offering pupils cash rewards for good attendance. Pupils who do not miss a single day in a year can earn up to £80.00. On the stick side, in Germany the electronics company Siemens has developed a tracker which can be sown into a school uniform or school bag which will use global positioning satellite technology and be able to pinpoint a truanting child to within five metres. But surveillance does not stop at getting pupils past the school gate. A school in Leeds wants to build a fish tank into a glass wall for the boys and girls lavatories so that staff can see into the washrooms and keep an eye on pupils hanging around outside the cubicles. It is interesting to note that the article in the TES which described this proposal made absolutely no mention of human rights issues.

Of course, when they get to school, they find an organisation which reflects elements of its historical origins in mass production, control and surveillance. Charles Handy, at the time a Professor of Business Organisations, turned his attention to secondary schools in the 1980s and concluded that the nearest model of organisational style he could come up with in analysing schools was *prisons,* in that the inmates' routine is disrupted every 40 minutes, they change their place of work and supervisors constantly, they have no place to call their own and they are often forbidden to communicate with each other. He also argued that if you look at schools in another way then they are more like *factories* and the pupils like products which are inspected at the end of the production line, sometimes rejected as sub-standard and then stamped 'Maths', 'English', 'History' and so on.

In England this situation has been made worse by the introduction of the national curriculum. A recent study of the actual operation of the national curriculum over a five year period involving 7,000 pupils, 250 teachers and the observation of 97 lessons in primary, secondary and tertiary educational institutions concluded that,

> "... *the national curriculum, in operation, enforced a limited course restricted to the rote-learning of subject-specific knowledge so that pupils may perform well in written tests of memory. It is my contention that this knowledge-based, assessment driven curriculum demands didactic drill-training to ensure examination success; and that such a pedagogy suppresses the development of a critical disposition, so that the school leaver becomes a passive serf or discontented outlaw, rather than an emancipated citizen or productive worker".*

It is not surprising then that there is pupil resistance to schooling. Indeed, it is perhaps surprising that there is not more resistance. One researcher I met had spent an entire year sitting in with a class of 14 year-olds in a Midlands school through every lesson they experienced. At the beginning of the year one of her research questions was *"why do pupils truant?"* At the end of a year of boredom, routine and irrelevance this question changed to *"why don't all pupils truant?"* And this was before the national curriculum. But resistance to schooling there is and resistance there always has been – sometimes violent resistance. Robert Adams in his fascinating book *Protests by Pupils* documents this in England and in many other countries, including the school strikes of 1911 which involved up to a *million* young people at one time.

In a survey of 15,000 British pupils carried out by the *Guardian* newspaper in 2001 some key findings were that the pupils felt that schools were not happy places, that pupils' views were not listened to, that they were not treated and respected as individuals and that schools were rigid, inflexible institutions. This strikes me as a root cause of a lot of pupil-teacher violence in schools today – **if you shut people up in a place they do not want to be, doing things they do not want to do often with only very uncertain and unclear prospects of personal benefit, then trouble will result.**

Bearing in mind this context of control, I now want to examine briefly in turn some of the specific ways in which schooling has been routinely involved in acts of physical and mental violence against children or helped to foster violence among children and hence the wider society. These will be physical punishment, gendered violence, stress and anxiety, militarisation and racism. I ought to say before I do this that these are merely brief illustrative examples selected from a great deal of documented evidence that I have gathered on pupils' violent experience of schooling over the last few years. What has really shocked me is how easy it has been to come across so much material so quickly.

1. Physical Punishment

The control and surveillance origins of formal schooling are reflected in its authoritarian nature. I have studied evidence from a wide range of countries in South and Central America, Africa, Asia, North America and Europe, and the one obvious conclusion is that, while there are some exceptions - particularly in Scandinavia and Holland - by far the predominant form of schooling internationally is authoritarian. A key element of these authoritarian relationships is the perceived right of teachers to punish, inherent in the need to maintain control and order. As one American writer put it,

"Systemic violence begins with the expectation that all students of similar ages should and can learn the same things. Children are placed with large groups of similarly aged students and teachers are forced to adopt methods of control and routine that would be better left to the military, the workforce or the penal system ... In a quest for conformity, students are monitored in their coming and

going, they are required to carry hall passes and must seek permission to leave the room. Their activities are directed and timed and their learning is scheduled into periods of work followed by short breaks. Such regimentation requires rules and punishment and administrative models that rely on differentiated power relations".

In terms of whether children in developing countries are better or worse off in school, it is interesting to note that a joint publication of the British Department for International Development and *Save the Children* recently and unusually noted that in some schools in a range of countries they studied (India, Mali, Lebanon, Liberia, Mozambique, Pakistan, Mongolia, Ethiopia and Peru),

"... it is almost certainly more damaging for children to be in school than out of it. Children whose days are spent herding animals rather than sitting in a classroom at least develop skills of problem solving and independence while the supposedly luckier ones in school are stunted in their mental, physical and emotional development by being rendered passive and having to spend hours each day in a crowded room under the control of an adult who punishes them for any normal level of activity such as moving or speaking".

Historically, this punishment has often taken the form of physical attack with a stick known as caning. It is salutary to note that evidence suggests that violent physical punishment of pupils in schools (beating, ear pulling, cheek pinching and the like) is still widespread in many parts of the world. I have found evidence of the common use of caning in Botswana, Palestine, South Africa, Colombia, Morocco, Japan, India, Thailand, Kenya, The Gambia, South Korea and the USA. Indeed it was only finally banned in all state schools in this country in 1986 and in schools altogether as late as 1999. Even then a survey of 1,000 parents in England and Wales in 2000 found that 51% thought that corporal punishment should be reintroduced in schools. This is despite overwhelming and consistent evidence that violence reproduces violence. A major review of international research by the Gulbenkian Foundation published in 1995, for example, concluded that,

> *"Research over the past 40 years has been remarkably consistent in showing that hitting children increases the chances of a child becoming physically aggressive, delinquent or both. The research in this book shows that corporal punishment leaves invisible scars that affect many aspects of life."*
> (Gulbenkian Foundation, 1995: 52).

2. Gender

In some societies the violence used to sustain power and control can be of a gendered nature. According to the South African Police Service, a woman is raped in South Africa about every 35 seconds. In South African schools sexual violence against females is correspondingly widespread. A recent report by Human Rights Watch on South African schools which was entitled *Scared at School* stated unambiguously that *"South African schoolgirls of every race and economic group daily encounter sexual violence and harassment that impedes their access to education. Girls are raped, sexually abused, sexually harassed and assaulted at school by male classmates and even teachers"*. In fact, it quotes a report by the Medical Research Council in 1998, which found that 37.7% of rape victims named their schoolteacher or school principal as the perpetrator. In case you think you misread me – over one third of rapes in South Africa are carried out by school teaching staff. The report also notes that the prevalence of sexual harassment is also based on psychological coercion. The report states,

> *"In some cases girls acquiesce to sexual demands from teachers because of fears that they will be physically punished if they refuse. In other cases, teachers abuse their position of authority by promising better grades or money in exchange for sex. In the worst cases, teachers operate within a climate of seeming entitlement to sexual favours from students. In a wide spectrum of cases, the school response is weak, nonexistent or actually facilitates continued abuse"* (2001: 42).

Insights, which is a bulletin published jointly by the Department for International Development and the Centre for International Education at the University of Sussex, found parallel phenomena on a widespread basis in Malawi, Uganda, Zimbabwe. Of course, in these contexts the added dimension of violence is the serious threat of the transmission of HIV/AIDS.

3. Stress and Anxiety

In some parts of the world there is increasing evidence of the psychological and physical harm - stress, anxiety and resulting physical symptoms - done to children and teachers internationally by increasingly controlled, regulated, ordered, inspected, competitive and test-driven schooling systems which are aimed at classification and ranking in order to serve markets in education. A survey of 8,000 pupils in England and Wales, for example, in 2000 found that stress is damaging pupils physical and emotional well being and is resulting in sleeping and eating disorders. The cause of this was endless testing, which is why the report was entitled *Tested to Destruction*. It calculated that by the time the average sixth former leaves school he or she will have taken 75 or more external tests.

In Germany last year the Bavarian Teachers' Federation warned of an alarming rise in the number of primary school pupils taking medication for stress or simply to improve school performance. One in five primary children in Germany is taking medication for these reasons, the union said, following surveys carried out by health authorities in southern Germany. Common symptoms were headaches, stomach aches, sleeplessness and loss of appetite. In India the Chair of the Central Board of Secondary Education called for an overhaul of the examination system to tackle the problem of student stress. In 2000, as in previous years, at least four suicides by failing students were reported. In a study done in America last year, which was actually designed to find out the good news about schools, it was found that students were stressed out and regularly participated in devious, deceptive and cruel behaviour to get the best grade possible. It quotes one 14 year-old as saying,

> *"High school is simply a way of building up tolerance for stress. School turns students into robots, just doing the routine."*

4. Militarisation

The use of child soldiers in wars has become increasingly common in recent years. However, in some societies schools themselves have been militarised. There have been a number of historical examples of this but here I shall just give some brief recent examples. Under the Khmer Rouge in Cambodia, as recently as the early 1990s, dominant aspects of the school curriculum for children as young as nine were how to lay landmines, set booby traps with explosives and to make explosives from fertilisers. In America, our great ally, John Ashcroft, President Bush's Attorney General, has publicly stated that he believes that the answer to America's school shootings such as that at Columbine High School in Colorado in 1999, is in **allowing pupils to be armed in the classroom**. In Venezuela President Chavez decreed in 1999 that all schoolchildren would be given military training which would involve weapons handling because it would make Venezuela more efficient. He announced this in a four hour speech to Venezuela's teacher union and it was received with a standing ovation. Ironically, the Venzuelan military held up as a model of discipline and efficiency were themselves later involved in illegal executions and beatings of civilians during the widespread flooding that hit Venezuela six months after this announcement.

5. Racism

Racial hatred and ethnic prejudice can also be actively promoted by an education system. I have already mentioned the examples of Nazi Germany, South Africa and Rwanda. In Israel and Palestine, strongly 'us and them' stances taken in school textbooks have helped to sustain distrust and hatred as have school systems in Serbia, Bosnia and Kosovo. A national report in India published in April 2002, stated that many lower caste or so-called 'untouchable' children are regularly beaten at school by teachers who regard them as polluting the class. Teachers in schools made them targets for their anger and abuse and they were punished at the slightest pretext and often humiliated. There are 200 million people of this caste in India. In an article on Cyprus that appeared during 2002, one Greek Cypriot at school in the 1970s stated that she had yet to forget the slogan *'the good Turk is the dead Turk'* two decades after it was drummed into her in the classroom. In the same article a fifteen-year-old said, *"Our teachers always say that everything is the fault of the Turks"*, while a Greek Cypriot school teacher who was himself active in peace and reconciliation nevertheless noted that, *"Usually whenever the word Turk or Turkish Cypriot is mentioned in state school classes, they are automatically associated with an act of barbarism. I see it with my own children who blame everything from a natural disaster to a car-crash on the Turks. What we are essentially fighting here is the mask of the devil we have painted on the other's face"*.

Schools are not, therefore, always or necessarily safe havens for young people and indeed can actually harm them and help to reproduce violence in the wider society. What there is not time to discuss here in any detail, but what ought to be at least mentioned, is the sin of omission, that is when schools ignore something violent that is happening and therefore help to reproduce it and there is also considerable evidence of this. One example for which there is considerable evidence is bullying in general and homophobic bullying in particular. I would also argue that, given the consistent evidence of widespread racism amongst British youth, and indeed the population in general, then the British education system, and the national curriculum in particular, has been guilty of helping to reproduce racism, both by omission and by failure to openly confront and analyse it in an overt and systematic manner.

So, as Lenin once put it, What is to be done? The first thing to be said is very simple – schools should stop doing harm. However, I want to move beyond the simple absence of *negative* experiences to look at what education ought to do – what should be the *positive* goals of education? Education for peace will be a key theme of the rest of the lecture.

Answers to questions concerning the improvement of education like 'better examination results', or 'better behaved pupils' or 'more effective schools' beg more questions than they answer as they tell you nothing about the philosophical and ideological context which is needed to judge words like 'better', 'examination', 'behaviour' and 'effective'. Even phrases like 'more flexibility', 'more creativity', 'more imagination', 'more independence' or 'more sense of enquiry', all of which I continue to argue for, are meaningless unless given an ideological context. Even happiness, a commodity in short supply in many formal education systems, is not context free. Let us take the example of a terrorist training camp. You could have a terrorist training regime which aimed to produce flexible, creative, imaginative and independent terrorists and did so. They may well also be very literate and numerate. And on top of that they may be happy and enjoy their training. Within its own goals it would have to be regarded as effective. But are the goals desirable? Are terrorists and terror a good thing to produce?

While it remains true that if we are forcing or pushing young people into schooling or other forms of education it ought at least to be enjoyable, interesting and relevant, there are nevertheless larger goals within which even these aims ought to be set. For me, and I think for my colleagues in the Centre for International Education and Research, **the twin fundamental goals of education should be peace and democracy**, which cannot be separated. These personal priorities stem partly from a long academic interest in the politics of sub-Saharan Africa, and the negative consequences that authoritarianism, war and violence have had on development there. However, such academic interests became very real and personal during my four year stay in South Africa. For a series of historical and sociological reasons, South Africa is a very violent society. During my time as Head of the Department of Education at the University of Natal, a temporary member of our staff and one of our PGCE students were both murdered. During a study I did of violence reduction in three schools, I turned up at a school to do an interview with a teacher minutes after he had been involved in a near fatal incident with a pupil with a loaded gun. So I have also learnt the paramount importance of peace and peaceful conflict resolution in a rather first hand way.

However, I would also argue that the achievement of more peaceful societies also requires the institutionalisation of greater levels of democracy than is currently the case globally. As Frederico Mayor, the former Director-General of UNESCO, put it,

"Lasting peace is a prerequisite for the exercise of human rights and duties. It is not the peace of silence, of men and women who by choice and constraint remain silent. It is the peace of freedom – and therefore of just laws – of happiness, equality and solidarity in which all citizens

count, live together and share. Peace, development and democracy form an interactive triangle".

Democracy provides the best environment available for the peaceful solution of disputes and conflicts. While democracies are far from being perfect, accountable and representative government minimizes internal violence and greatly decreases the possibility of going to war without good reason. At the micro level of social institutions such as the workplace or the school, if they are organised democratically then there is an emphasis on the peaceful solution of problems and disagreements through discussion and participation, rather than imposition, confrontation, conflict and violence.

Democracy, however, is not possible without democrats. Democracy is only sustainable in a supportive political culture where a sufficient proportion of the population has a high commitment to democratic values, skills and, particularly, behaviours. This is based on an understanding of democracy that goes beyond the minimum ritual of voting (or not voting) every four or five years in an election. While democracy does require an informed citizenry capable of making genuine political choices, it also requires a fuller and **deeper notion of democracy** that forms the basis of a democratic society in which **people actually behave in a democratic manner in their daily interactions**. What are the characteristics of such a person? Somebody described as democratic would, for example, celebrate social and political diversity, work for and practice mutual respect between individuals and groups, regard all people as having equal social and political rights as human beings, respect evidence in forming their own opinions and respect the opinions of others based on evidence, be open to changing one's mind in the light of new evidence and possess a critical and analytical stance towards information. The democratic citizen would possess a proclivity to reason, open-mindedness and fairness and the practice of co-operation, bargaining, compromise and accommodation.

If education is to help to foster and develop such characteristics, then its organisation should reflect democracy in its daily practices as democratic values and behaviours are learned as much by experience as by hearing or reading about them.

Education should offer opportunities for democratic participation and for the learning of democratic political skills and values in practice in terms of institutional and curriculum organisation. Yet contemporary formal schooling is an authoritarian experience for many and a violent, damaging and dehumanising experience for some. Power and authority over what is learned, when, where and how is not with learners and, in many cases, not even with teachers. This is despite article 12 of the UN Convention of the Rights of the Child which says that children have the right to express an opinion, and to have that opinion taken into account, in any matter or procedure affecting the child. Modern mass schooling systems are not on the whole contributing to the development of more democratic and peaceful individuals and societies and indeed were not primarily designed to do in the first place. There is no single, perfect means of organising learning. Any system or vehicle of provision of education can be used for good or bad purposes. For example, distance-based education, the internet, religious schools and even normally progressive alternatives such as home-based education, flexischooling and small schools can all potentially be used to foster either greater peace and democracy or authoritarianism, bigotry and potential violence.

Educational provision needs to be designed to meet the needs and specific contexts of children, rather than children having to fit into 'one size fits all' versions of formal schooling, wherever they are and whoever they are. For example, refugee children, street children, special needs children, nomadic children, children in post-conflict societies, orphaned children, children in very poor housing areas in big cities and children in rural areas in developing countries all have widely differing needs and problems that cannot be met by one form of standardised provision. Their needs have to be accurately identified through research and discussion with them and appropriate education designed accordingly. So, on the one hand I am arguing for a post-modern recognition of human diversity and a rejection of modernist 'iron law' thinking in which one form of standardised, conventional schooling is seen as good for everybody. On the other hand, however, and in opposition to some forms of post-modern relativism, education must give overall priority to education for democracy and human rights.

I want to end with a comment from an American official of that hard-headed citadel of global capitalism and scourge of developing countries, the World Bank in Washington. At first he advocated vouchers to maximise user choice. But he changed his mind:

"In the case of Russia, I have been working in an ethnically heterogeneous federal system, much like our own, but falling apart. More than 100 ethnic groups now may control schools and, not having the traditional restraints, may now be able – if they choose – to teach disrespect for the rights of their neighbours. **Schools can contribute to Armageddon** *and I have been forced to learn that there are things in life – such as civil unrest and civil war – which are more expensive and important than an inefficient and cumbersome public education system."*

He asks, *"What is there that makes an education system essential for a consensus of democratic values and for the creation of a democratic society?"*

These are good questions and should be first order priorities in education. We do have quite a number of well-researched and recorded examples of democratic education and education for peace at a series of levels - whole education systems, individual schools and teachers, educational projects, non-governmental organisations and in home-based education and other forms of learning. We need to put these at the top of educational agendas and to learn from them so as to build an education that actively promotes democracy and peace rather than contributing to their opposites.

* * * * *

See: Harber, Clive (2004) *Schooling as Violence*, Routledge Falmer

Postscript: beyond damage limitation - teaching in the next learning system ...

Teachers will of course have much to unlearn and much to learn. Nor will it be easy for them to find appropriate help and guidance. There will be things for them to do, directions for which are given in no current manual of pedagogy. Here are some of them:

- to efface themselves as much as possible,
- to realise that not the teachers, but the children, play the leading part in the drama of learning,
- to put unbounded faith in the nature of children, in spite of its early weaknesses, crudities, and other shortcomings,
- to feel sure that its higher tendencies, if allowed to unfold themselves in due season, will gradually master and control the lower,
- to give children as much freedom as is compatible with the maintenance of the reality rather than the semblance of order,
- to relieve children from the deadening pressure of the discipline of drill, and to help them to achieve the discipline of self-control,
- to provide outlets for all their healthy activities, taking care that these shape their own channels, as far as may be possible, and are not merely directed into ready-made canals,
- to place at their disposal such materials as will provide them both with mental and spiritual food, and with opportunities for the exercise of their mental and spiritual faculties,
- to give them such guidance as their expanding natures may seem to need, taking care that the guidance given is the outcome of sympathetic study of their instinctive tendencies, and interferes as little as possible with their freedom of choice,
- to do nothing for them which they can reasonably be expected to do for themselves,

- to abstain from that excessive fault-finding which the dogmatic spirit (always prone to mistake correctness for goodness) is apt to engender, and which paralyses children's initiative, and makes them morbidly self-conscious and self-distrustful,
- to help them to think more of overcoming difficulties, and doing things well, than of producing plausible and possibly deceptive results,
- to foster their natural sincerity, and keep far away from them whatever savours of make-believe, self-deception, and fraud,
- to study and take thought for their individuality, so that they may realise and outgrow themselves and at last transcend their individuality, in their own particular way, the way which Nature seems to have marked out as best for them,
- to help them to develop all their expansive instincts, so that their growth may be as many-sided and therefore as healthy and harmonious as possible,
- to realise, and help them to realise (should this be necessary), that healthy and harmonious growth is its own reward, and so relieve them from the false and demoralising stimulus of external rewards and punishments,
- to discourage competition between child and child, with the vanity and selfishness which this necessarily tends to breed,
- to foster the children's communal instinct, their spirit of comradeship, their latent capacity for sympathy and love.

I could easily make this list longer, but I think I have made it long enough. Perhaps I have made it too long, for after all it is an idea that I am setting before the teachers of the future, not a theory, still less a fully elaborated system. If the idea commends itself to teachers in any respect or degree, they must interpret it (both in theory and practice) in their own individual way. I should be false to my own first principles if I tried to do for them what, if it is to have any lasting value, they must do for themselves.

Lightly edited version of an extract from Edmond Holmes, Chief Inspector of Schools, in The Tragedy of Education, (1911) p.73.